Machine Learning With Python

A Practical Guide for Experts

Travis Booth

or indirect, that are incurred as a result of the use of information contained within this document, including, but not limited to, errors, omissions, or inaccuracies.

Books by Travis Booth

Scan the Code to Learn More

Machine Learning Series

Machine Learning With Python: Hands-On Learning for Beginners

Machine Learning With Python: An In Depth Guide Beyond the Basics

Python Data Analytics Series

Python Data Analytics: The Beginner's Real World Crash Course

Python Data Analytics: A Hands-On Guide Beyond the Basics

Python Data Science Series

Python Data Science: Hands-On Learning for Beginners

Python Data Science: A Hands-On Guide Beyond the Basics

Deep Learning Series

Deep Learning With Python: A Hands-On Guide for Beginners

Deep Learning With Python: A Comprehensive Guide Beyond the Basics

Bonus Offer: Get the Ebook absolutely free when you purchase the paperback via Kindle Matchbook!

Table Of Contents

Introduction

Chapter 1: Recap: Machine Learning Basics

Learning Algorithms

Performance Measure

Experiences

Reinforcement Learning

Creating a Learning Problem

Comparing Learning Models

Solving Reinforcement Learning Problems

Implementing Reinforcement Learning

Chapter 2: Information Theory and Probability

Importance of Probability

Sources of Uncertainty

Random Variables

Probabilistic Distribution

Conditional Probability

Conditional Probability Chain Rules

Covariance, Variance and Expectations

Chapter 3: Computations in Machine Learning

Rounding Errors

Inappropriate Conditioning

The Softmax Function

Comparing Sigmoid and Softmax Functions

Chapter 4: Machine Learning for Financial Engineering

Importance of Machine Learning in Finance

Machine Learning Applications in Finance

Implementing Machine Learning in Finance

Chapter 5: Machine Learning for Spam Filtration

Applying Bayes Rule

Chapter 6: Machine Learning for Sentiment Analysis

Word Transformation

Determining Relevance

Training a Regression Model

Analyzing Large Datasets

Chapter 7: Natural Language Processing

History of Natural Language Processing

NLP In Machine Learning

Stop Words and Tokenization

Bag of Words Model (BoW)

CountVectorizer

Term Frequency Inverse Document Frequency (TFIDF)

Chapter 8: Loading Machine Learning Models into Real World Applications

Model Training

Data Storage in SQLite

Building Web Apps

Converting Classifiers into Web Apps

Conclusion

References

Introduction

The industrial revolution sparked changes in the history of mankind, changes that would go on to influence the future of the world. Since then, inventors and researchers have worked towards a dream of building machines that can think like humans do. Unknown to many, this history dates back to ancient Greece. Tales of Pandora and Galatea reveal that the allure of an artificial life is not a preserve of our modern world. In their studies and work, early mythological inventors like Hephaestus and Daedalus had already laid the foundations into studies that would eventually lead us to this point in time.

By the time the earliest programmable computers became a reality, the thought of these devices becoming ever so intelligent wasn't on the horizon for many people. After all, these were simple computers that performed simple tasks. As we know, human needs and wants are dynamic. The simplicity around the tasks performed by the earliest computers wasn't going to last. As our demands grew, so did the need to push the limits of computers.

Today, we live in the era of artificial intelligence. Much as this is a laudable fact, we are still years away from realizing the true potential of combining machine efficiency with the immense depth of human imagination. Artificial intelligence is currently one of the most thriving fields any programmer would wish to delve into, and for a good reason - this is the future!

From research topics to projects and applications in different stages of production, there is a lot going on in the world of machine learning. We encounter these devices on a daily basis. Think about medical diagnostics, automation of mundane and repetitive labor tasks, speech and facial recognition; all these highlight the fact that we live in interesting times. Each day we encounter these machines, they embed deeper into our lives and become part of our experience, and existence. This is machine learning.

The concept of machine learning is so explicit, it's a self-defining discipline. Simply put, it is about teaching machines to think and make decisions as we would. The difference between the way machines learn and the way we do is that while for the most part we learn from experiences, machines learn from data. You don't expect to take your computer to kindergarten to learn the vowels, sing Baby Shark, and probably go for P.E classes, right?

Data forms the core of machine learning because within data, therein lies a lot of truths, truths whose depths exceed our imagination. The computations machines can perform on data are incredible, beyond anything a human brain could do. Just as we learn by building on our experiences and compounding knowledge, so do machines with data. Once we introduce data to a machine learning model, we must create an environment where we update the data stream frequently. This builds the machine's learning ability. The more data machine learning models are exposed to, the easier it is for these models to expand their potential.

Artificial intelligence systems can hardly depend on hard-coded knowledge. For this reason, they must obtain their knowledge by extracting data from different databases. It is this capacity that forms the core of machine learning. Through machine learning, computers can now solve problems that demand knowledge of our world and even make subjective suggestions and decisions.

Machine learning is not just about adding data to the model. It is also about providing sufficient resources to enable the model to scale up operations. Building sufficient memory and other hardware resources is a mandatory prerequisite for successful machine learning. During the infant stages of machine learning, computers were built to solve problems that were relatively difficult for humans to handle, but easier for machines. Most of these were challenges involving machine rules and formal math problems. However, the challenge that we encountered with machines back in the day was that they were unable to solve problems that were easy for us to do, but difficult for us to explain.

Given the challenge above, the need for intuitive solutions that could help overcome this problem meant helping computers learn from building experiences. This way, they would see the world in a different construct, a conceptual hierarchy. The hierarchy of concepts meant that computers could soon interpret events on their own, and perform tasks without a human operator.

Building on this hierarchical concept, computers were also programmed to learn by compounding knowledge of simpler concepts and using this to solve complex assignments. This ushered in deep learning.

In the earlier books in this series, deep learning and machine learning have been discussed in-depth, citing introductory concepts that give you basic foundational ideas. In line with the machine learning culture, we build onto what we learned earlier in the series in this book. Since most of the basic concepts were discussed already, this book will focus on the advanced knowledge of Python in machine learning. We will tackle complex assignments and give you a real-world experience of machine learning at work in different environments.

We are building machines that can solve real world problems, and to do that, we must be able to communicate with the machines in a language they understand. This is where scripting languages like Python come in handy. There are many other languages that you can use for programming in machine learning, each with their unique features, benefits, and constraints. However, you probably know already that the Python library is one of the most diverse, extensive, and easy-to-use resources any developer needs for programming in machine learning. The benefits of using Python outweigh those of using any other programming language, and this is why we focus on Python.

Does this mean the other programming languages are dead? No, that is not the case. As an expert developer, it is wise to master Python, but at the same time learn other programming languages because in your career, you will encounter different developer environments where teams predominantly use specific programming languages apart from Python. You need to be versatile. The good thing with mastering Python, however, is that your skills and competency are universal. You can easily walk into any development team and work together like you have been with them for years.

Chapter 1: Recap: Machine Learning Basics

As we delve into the intrigues of machine learning, it is important that we highlight that this is an expansive subject whose boundaries keep expanding over time. As a subset of artificial intelligence, the moment you start reading about machine learning, you can expect to find your way into deep learning and further into artificial intelligence, too. Many concepts are shared across the board among these three subjects, so knowledge in one will make your work easier if at a later date you want to learn about another.

In the earlier books in this series you covered introductory concepts in machine learning. In this chapter, we will remind ourselves of the important basics that will guide you in machine learning.

Learning Algorithms

An algorithm in machine learning is a program that is written to learn from data. A computer program can learn from an experience according to some assignments, performance measures, and its ability to perform the tasks set out for it. In the course of this learning exercise, the computer should improve its experience and understanding of the concepts learned.

In machine learning, we allow computers to perform assignments that are too difficult for us to solve using the normal programs that we write or design. Most of these programs are specific and can only return results specific to the questions we ask. They cannot go beyond the limit of their programming.

In the course of machine learning, computers are asked to perform specific tasks to return the results we need. Some of the tasks that computers perform include the following:

- **Classification**

This is a situation where we ask the computer to specify the category a specific input belongs. In order to perform such tasks, learning algorithms must produce functions in the following syntax:

$$f: Rn \rightarrow \{1, \ldots, k\}$$

Building up on this, the function y = f(x) assigns the vector x as the input in the function, which is then classified under a category represented by y in the function described.

All the other variables in the function, like f, represent a distribution probability output for any number of classes.

- **Computing missing inputs in classification**

In the example above, the machine learning program is dealing with a situation where all variants in the function are provided. However, this is not always the case. You will come across situations where there is no guarantee that all the input vectors are available. This is one of the challenging experiences that necessitate machine learning.

To handle such a scenario, the algorithm will initially identify and conclusively define one function upon which it will map outputs based on specific categorical instructions.

If you are missing some inputs, the computer will no longer provide just one classification function as outlined in the first example. Instead, you will have a set of functions, each of which the algorithm must learn and interpret correctly.

Each of the functions presented must correlate to the original classifier (x), but with several inputs missing. What we have here is a common problem in the health sector, especially when diagnosing diseases. More often, researchers have to perform several tests to determine the outcome. These tests are very invasive and often expensive. An alternative way to proceed is through probabilistic distribution. In this case, the researchers consider all the possible variables that are relevant to the study, then handle the classification problem by eliminating all the missing values.

- **Regression**

A regression algorithm is specifically tasked with predicting the next possible outcome in a numerical value set, when a specific input is provided. In this situation, the learning algorithm is tasked with determining the output for problems with the following function syntax:

$$f : Rn \rightarrow R$$

While this function is similar to classification algorithm functions, the difference is in the nature and format of the output. Regression algorithms are often used when determining the expected claim an insured person will make, especially when determining the appropriate insurance premiums. Regression algorithms are also used in the financial markets to determine the possible price of securities given a specific input. This is the backbone of algorithmic trading.

- **Transcription**

Transcription algorithms demand that machine learning models study an unstructured data set and transcribe it into understandable text. These algorithms are often used in optical character recognition (OCR) systems. In this case, you show the computer some pictures that contain text, and in return, the computer transcribes and returns a text document either in Unicode or ASCII format.

This is a common phenomenon in offices, where data entry clerks process lots of pdf documents. Google Street View is another example of a company that uses this process to determine addresses. Street addresses are captured in images, but through the transcription algorithm, it can interpret them and send instructions on text.

- **Translation**

In the case of translation, the machine learning model is fed input in textual format, but in a foreign language. Based on this input, the computer will then translate it into the desired language through a sequence of symbols. This is perhaps one of the most frequently used forms of machine learning today. Many websites have this feature turned on and you might not even have to explicitly request for the website to be translated. If you open a website written in Mandarin, the translation algorithm automatically translates the content into English or your preferred language.

- **Structured output algorithms**

In this type of assignment, the output we expect from the machine learning model is a vector. This basically means the machine returns data structures that contain multitudes of values. Your model must then establish the important relationships between each of the elements important to your query. Structured output assignments are wide, wider than any of the algorithm classes we have looked at. In some cases it includes translation and transcription.

A good example of structured output algorithms in use is parsing. This is a situation where you map a natural language sentence in a tree such that you can determine the grammatical context of that sentence. From this tree, you will have nodes that identify grammar features like adverbs, nouns, and verbs.

Tasks performed in this algorithm are called structured output assignments because your machine learning model will generally return several values, all of which share a complex but intimate association. Take the example of using an OCR. Once the machine learning model identifies the content, the words it returns must form a credible sentence.

- **Anomaly detection**

If you are aware of fraud detection programs in your company or at the bank, this is the algorithm that they run. What happens in this scenario is that the model will run through several objects or events, and flag those that are atypical to the normal instructions. Your credit card company will, for example, monitor your spending habits such that if you generally spend no more than $100 on shopping, a transaction of $5,602 will be flagged for further review.

If someone steals your credit card and your personal information, their purchases and activities on that card will be skewed so far from your normal distribution. If the credit card company realizes this, they can lock the account pending further investigation, in the process protecting your account, even without your request or awareness.

- **Sampling and synthesis**

This is a learning model where the computer is tasked with producing new samples that are similar to the samples used in training. This kind of algorithm is used in situations where generating repetitive but similar content is necessary, especially if you are dealing with media files. Performing these tasks by hand would be near-impossible, painstaking and a horrendous waste of time.

If you are a gamer, you experience this all the time. Video games do not create pixels all the time. They simply use the training data to generate new scenes by repeating landscapes and large objects within the game.

- **Imputation**

You first encountered imputation in data handling. It is an important process for managing missing values in a dataset. For data analysts, this is one of the most important steps in making sure they get the correct outcome.

In an imputation algorithm, learning takes place in the following format:

$$x \in R^n$$

However, some entries for x might be unavailable. In this case, the algorithm will have to compute possible values for the missing input.

- **Denoising**

This is a unique example where the machine learning model is fed a corrupted sample in the following format;

$$\tilde{x} \quad R^n$$

This data is obtained through an unknown corruption process, but the machine is tasked with delivering a clean data sample in the format below:

$$x \in R^n$$

The role of the computer is not just delivering the output, but it must also determine the clean sample from the corrupted sample. More importantly, the task is to identify the conditional probability distribution in the following format:

$$p(x \mid \tilde{x})$$

There are several other tasks that machine learning models perform. However, these are the most common tasks you will come across when working with or building models all the time.

Performance Measure

To determine the effectiveness of any machine learning algorithm, or model for that matter, we must have a quantitative performance measure. This measure must be specific and relative to the assignment you expect the algorithm or model to perform. In the case of classification and transcription assignments, the performance measure is the accuracy of the machine learning model. This refers to the output portion that is produced as correct values by the model.

Other information we can get from this is the rate of error. This identifies how much of the output is incorrect. The rate of error is often referred to as the expected 0-1 loss. What this means is that for any sample, if the classification is correct, the expected loss is 0, but if the classification is incorrect, the expected loss is 1.

Assuming you are working on assignments like estimating the density of some population, error rates, accuracy measures or any other 0-1 loss estimates are not applicable. For such an example you would need a performance measure that identifies the continuous nature of the data sample, and assign a value-based score for every example.

In machine learning, one of the key considerations is to determine how well the model will perform against data samples that it has not been introduced to before. This is an important consideration because it tells us how well the system will perform in the real world where we cannot control input. For this purpose, we need quality test samples different from the samples used in building and training the machine learning model.

Looking at performance measures in this manner reveals a simplistic approach, mainly an objective process. However, this is not always the case. In the real world, choosing a performance measure is difficult. The chosen measure must bear correlation with the preferred behavior you expect of the model you are building.

Such concerns arise in many cases because you are uncertain about what the model is built to measure. Say you are working on a transcription assignment, for example. Do we choose the performance measure as the system's accuracy at transcription, or do we choose a performance measure that we can appreciate by virtue of the fact that it managed to get some features of our sequence right?

Both options are doable, but which one holds more value? Machine learning is not just about delivering results, it is about value addition in the results delivered. Let's look at another example to help you understand this further. If we are working on a regression algorithm, should we consider the system a failure if it hardly makes grave mistakes, or if it makes small to medium-sized mistakes all the time?

Focusing on the two examples above, the selection choice will, therefore, depend on the type of project you are building, and what you need it to do. There are cases where you already know how much quantity you need to measure in a given machine learning model. However, measuring the data as you intend to would not be feasible. If you are working on a probabilistic model, you might have realized by now that most of these models only give an implicit representation of the probabilistic distribution of data samples. It is not feasible to determine the exact value assigned to a specific point in the model. If you look at such a scenario, it makes sense to come up with a unique performance measure that meets your objectives in as far as design is concerned, or a performance measure that gets you close enough.

Experiences

When we talk about experiences in machine learning, we allude to the type of learning. In the earlier books in this series you discussed this under supervised and unsupervised learning models. This concept defines the type of experience the model is built to have as it learns from data and interaction with users.

A good number of the learning algorithms used in this book follow a single dataset experience model. One dataset might contain any number of examples upon which the model will train and learn from. These examples are also referred to as data points.

In unsupervised learning models, the experience your model comes across is with a dataset that has multidimensional features. From this dataset, the model must then determine the important features and properties. Some of the tasks that are performed in this case include denoising, synthesis, or clustering. Clustering is one of the common tasks, given that the algorithm will categorize the data into bits based on subcategories, and group them accordingly.

In a supervised learning model, the algorithms have a different experience with datasets in that while the dataset contains specific features, every example in the dataset shares a close relationship with a target (label). Let's use one of the oldest datasets to explain this, the Iris dataset. In the Iris dataset, the annotation is according to the unique iris plant species. However, if you are using a supervised learning algorithm, your model will study the dataset and probably group the plants into species based on their length.

So what is the difference in experience between supervised and unsupervised learning? In unsupervised learning, the model studies more than one sample of a given vector (x) so it can learn whether there exists an explicit or implicit probabilistic distribution $p(x)$. The model might also attempt to determine whether there exists any properties of the distribution that are uniquely interesting.

In the case of supervised learning, the machine learning model will look at as many samples as possible of the random vector (x) and study the features of another random vector (y) then use the knowledge gained to determine how to predict vector x from vector y. This prediction takes the estimation format $p(x \backslash y)$.

From the explanation above, we can also derive the meaning of supervised and unsupervised learning. In supervised learning, the instructor provides a target y that teaches the machine learning model what it must do. On the other hand, unsupervised learning is a learning process devoid of instructor input. Once it is built and deployed, the machine must figure out how to make sensible predictions from data on its own.

By design, supervised and unsupervised learning models are not formal concepts as they are widely assumed to be. This is because we have many machine learning algorithms that can perform tasks across the divide.

What does this mean? If we follow the chain rule as stipulated in probability, it is possible to solve unsupervised problems of a $p(x)$ model by splitting the unsupervised learning problem into as many supervised learning problems as we see fit. At the same time, to solve a supervised learning problem of the nature $p(y \mid x)$, we can simply use unsupervised learning methods to determine the joint distribution $p(x, y)$.

Therefore, while these two learning methods are not necessarily distinct, they help us determine what algorithms do by classifying them accordingly. We can also have other variants of these learning models, like semi-supervised learning and multi-instance learning. Let us introduce experiences from the perspective of reinforcement learning.

While supervised and unsupervised learning models experience data in the form of a fixed dataset, reinforcement learning models go the extra mile, and experience the entire environment. This is a different approach that introduces the concept of feedback loops between the machine learning model and the experience ecosystem. This is a highly advanced concept that we will not discuss at this level.

In summary, many machine learning models basically experience datasets. We can define the datasets in so many ways, with the obvious definition being design matrices. A design matrix contains unique samples in every row. Columns in a design matrix, on the other hand, must correspond to a specific feature of the objects defined.

To illustrate this with the Iris dataset that contains 150 samples, each with four features, we can extrapolate the following function for our design matrix:

$$x \in R^{150 \times 4}$$

Just a fair reminder before we proceed, you must describe every sample as a vector, and each of the vectors must be similar in size. This is the precondition for defining a dataset as a design matrix. Unfortunately, in most cases this is impossible. A good example is a situation where you have a dataset with several students, with different preferences in the food and drinks they like. Each student will have a different BMI after lunch, so it is impossible to use the same vector to define all the students.

Earlier in the series, you were introduced to supervised and unsupervised learning as two distinct divides in machine learning. However, at this juncture you realize that there really isn't a formal difference between these two. In the same way, we cannot find a definitive taxonomy to set apart experiences and datasets. Most of the structures you will work with are intertwined between the two.

Reinforcement Learning

How do you learn a new skill? This is one of the biggest questions that many scientists have to grapple with from time to time. By learning how humans learn new skills, the same knowledge has been applied to machines through different approaches, which have resulted in the current developments in as far as artificial intelligence and machine learning are concerned.

We might not really have a definite explanation for why we do the things we do, or how we learn them, but we can come close in an attempt to explain some concepts. The basic element of learning is that we must interact with an environment in some way. Such interactions mean that we will grasp new concepts on a trial and error basis, until we realize what is good for us and what is bad. This is the same learning process that machines are put through, hence the success in machine learning.

A history of machine learning reveals some rudimentary steps in the earliest models. These models made several errors initially, but have since morphed into some of the most advanced models capable of solving problems we can only imagine. Reinforcement learning is an aspect of machine learning that focuses on the end result. All interactions with the environment in question are on the basis of specific expected goals.

In light of recent progress made in machine learning, it is safe to say that reinforcement learning models have an infinite potential in terms of what they can learn about us. We keep advancing and changing our needs, tastes and preferences, so machines that address these specifics must also change accordingly.

Creating a Learning Problem

Reinforcement learning is concerned with how we can create solutions to solve problems based on our actions. The final outcome is meant to increase the likelihood of a positive result. Since machines do not enjoy the sentimental benefits we do from positive results, rewards for machine learning models are created in the form of a numerical signal.

The learning model does not receive instructions on the specific actions they should engage. As a result, the model must engage the relevant participants in its immediate environment, and from there, determine the best course of action that delivers the utmost positive integral outcome.

To explain how machines learn, we will use the example of a baby learning how to walk. When a child is born, they cannot walk. However, they are constantly surrounded by people who move around freely, and as their brains develop, they realize the need to do the same. When the child comes of age, they can stand up on their legs. This makes them even more excited because they are learning something new and are excited about what comes next.

Of course, there will be falls and tumbles here and there, but this does not stop the child from learning. As the child learns, one thing that is also evident in their attempts is the fact that they will keep trying to learn from what they see you doing. The moment they realize they can walk, they will want to learn how to move faster.

Before your child learns how to walk, however, we skipped an important part - they must stand up. This is an obvious challenge, but one that they must overcome. The benefit for your child in the struggle to stand up is that when they do, they will finally be able to walk as you do.

The next thing your child will do after standing up is to try and stay still. They might need support from around them, but when they eventually get this right, this will be their favorite activity, especially when they notice you are around. The learning process continues.

Soon the child will learn how to walk. And from there, learn many other things along the way until they turn into adults. This is the natural learning curve for all humans. The same approach applies in reinforcement learning.

This process cannot happen overnight. Machines must learn and train on different sets of data until they perfect their tasks. We can look at the baby learning example in a formal construct, so that we identify the important aspects of reinforcement learning. Our problem statement in machine learning is similar to the baby's need to walk. The environment in machine learning is similar to the platform upon which the baby tries to walk, while the baby is our learning agent.

Different actions are involved in the machine learning process, which are similar to the baby's attempt to walk. Each step the baby makes is a step towards the final outcome. In machine learning, these steps are referred to as states. A reward system is also important so that the child can realize they have done something good. A reward system might be clapping for the baby, or giving them their favorite play toy. Since we cannot give our machine learning model a toy to play with, our reward scheme is a positive output.

Comparing Learning Models

Two learning models have been extensively discussed in as far as machine learning is concerned - supervised and unsupervised learning. In this section, we will compare these two with reinforcement learning as shown below.

- **Reinforcement learning vs. Supervised learning**

Supervised learning models do not feature external supervisory agents. The supervisory agent usually is knowledgeable about the learning environment and can share their knowledge with the machine learning model to improve its performance. However, in application we usually encounter specific challenges that might not be feasible for such a learning process. Case in point, we might end up with problems that demand more combinations to solve the problem than we imagined.

A good example of this is a game of chess. When the game starts, there are thousands of moves that can be played by each user. With each move, the probabilities change, so it is impossible to have a supervising agent at this point. Therefore, it is impractical to have a supervisory role in this type of learning environment.

Building a knowledge base upon which our model can learn is generally a futile approach. The best solution is to create a model that can teach itself based on its unique experiences with every learning agent it comes across. It is not just a learning curve, the model also gains and trains itself from these models.

This is the primary difference between reinforcement learning and supervised machine learning. The similarity between these two approaches is that they require that we map the difference between input and output variables. At the same time, however, the reinforcement learning reward scheme features a feedback loop agent that rewards positive results, which is not the case with supervised machine learning.

- **Reinforcement learning vs. Unsupervised learning**

As we have seen above, we must map the output and input variables in reinforcement learning. This process, however, is not applicable in unsupervised learning. Instead of mapping, unsupervised learning models learn by looking for trends and patterns in the learning process.

Assuming that you build a model that suggests new fashion news items to an audience, the model will learn by identifying stories that the user has read in the past, and use this to filter recommendations and make accurate suggestions.

A reinforcement learning model, on the other hand, will seek the audience's feedback by recommending several fashion news items to them. Based on the user's feedback, this model will then create its unique knowledge parameter to determine the kind of fashion news items that the audience prefers.

We also have semi-supervised learning which is a learning model that brings together supervised and unsupervised learning models. The difference between this and reinforcement learning is that it directly maps outcomes.

Solving Reinforcement Learning Problems

The simplest way to understand and solve reinforcement learning problems is to consider a slot machine at the casino. There are several machines available at any given time, each varying payout models. As a gamer, your intention is to get the highest possible payouts from the machines. The challenge is how to go about this.

A rudimentary approach would be to choose a single machine that you fancy and spend most of the day trying your luck at the levers. You might hit the jackpot, but the chances of this happening are stacked against you. In fact, for the most part you will waste a lot of money in the process. This is what is referred to as the pure exploitation method, and just in case you are thinking about it, it is not the best approach to maximize your outcome.

Another option is to consider a pure exploration method. In this case, you will pull the lever in every single slot machine, hoping that one of them hits the jackpot. It is also a rudimentary approach, and you might not hit the jackpot.

However, you have a better chance of winning than using the pure exploitation approach.

None of the approaches explained above are optimal, to say the least. You need a solution that will overcome the exploitation vs exploration challenge in reinforcement learning.

One suitable approach is the Markov Decision Process. Before we solve the problem, we must first identify the framework, determine the possible approaches, and choose the optimal approach from the list.

The Markov decision process is a mathematical construct that addresses reinforcement learning in the following elements:

- Value (V)
- Policy
- Reward function (R)
- States (S)
- Actions (A)

To move from the initial state (S) to the final state (S¹), we must make a transformational action (A). Each time we perform an action, we expect a reward. As a result, the desire for better rewards will push us towards either a positive or negative reward.

All actions performed determine the nature of the policy in place and the type of rewards that we use in the process. The rewards eventually determine the value we look forward to. The emphasis here, therefore, is to make sure that we can maximize the rewards by choosing the optimal policy.

Another solution is to use the shortest path approach. In this system, we try to find the easiest route between the starting point and the ending point. As we do that, our aim is to arrive at the end point using the lowest possible cost.

To determine whether the policy we use is a pure exploitation or pure exploration approach, we need to first understand that we are not using an optimal policy. An optimal policy would be free of errors. However, in a probabilistic problem, there must be an element of uncertainty. We can go about this by looking at the following possibilities:

- In the first case, we use an action based approach where our emphasis lies in determining the best action to perform at every step from the beginning to the end.
- The second option is a value based approach where our emphasis is on the cumulative reward we hope to achieve when we arrive at the end point.
- The final approach is a policy based system where we try to choose the best policy that can get us to the final point.

Implementing Reinforcement Learning

To implement reinforcement learning, one of the best algorithms that can derive the right outcome is the Q-learning algorithm. This is a policy approach where we use a neural network as the function approximator. This algorithm has often been used extensively in the world of gaming, where machine learning models beat human players by studying their moves, and creating a model to outplay them.

The learning process for this algorithm is as follows:

First, the model will determine the nature of values present in the learning environment. From there, it will study the present state then determine an action path for each state. This is done for all states. Finally, the algorithm will settle on the appropriate reward and the relevant state.

From here, it updates its values for the state based on the maximum rewards possible, and the output for the following state. The machine learning model will then update itself and repeat this process until it arrives at the necessary terminal point.

Chapter 2: Information Theory and Probability

Information and probability theories play an important role in machine learning. Probability is a mathematical concept that we use to determine the level of certainty of an event or a statement. When dealing with probability theories, we look at the possibility of quantifying the level of uncertainty in the event happening. In machine learning, probability is used to inform us how the models we build will make decisions by reasoning with the data they are exposed to. For this reason, we work around algorithms that determine outcomes based on probabilities. Probability is also used in machine learning to understand why our model behaves the way it does.

Probability is not just confined to math and artificial intelligence, it is an important part of engineering and other scientific disciplines. Through probability, we can understand why some statements are the way they are, and use information theory to support our ability to quantify the level of uncertainty in a probabilistic problem.

Importance of Probability

Why is it important to study probability in the context of machine learning? A lot of scientific disciplines are confined to certain and deterministic studies. For example, when you want to write some code, the assumption is that your computer will perform the operation just as you laid it out in the instructions. While there is always the possibility of an error in execution, or the code you write, most programs are written without error because the dev teams take their time to go through the code and make sure it is perfect. With this in mind, therefore, many applications are hardly written with the possibility of accounting for errors in mind.

In machine learning, uncertainties are part of the work you do. You will have to work with deterministic and non-stochastic quantities from time to time, hence the need for in-depth knowledge of probability theories. The level of uncertainty introduced into a machine learning model might arise from any source, most of which are unknown.

Probabilities affect virtually any activity that we engage in. If we eliminate mathematical propositions that are by definition true or false, it is almost impossible to come across a situation where the outcome is always free of uncertainty. Guarantees in real life are almost impossible to find. There must be an element of uncertainty that affects a given outcome, and this is why probability is important in machine learning.

Machine learning generally attempts to integrate computers into our lives by learning how we do things from interacting with data. Humans are near-perfect, but never perfect. It follows that for machines to make decisions and act in such a manner that suggests the closest semblance to human decision making, we must bring probability into the picture.

Sources of Uncertainty

Uncertainty is common in many a situation. You have to factor in this possibility to arrive at a feasible solution. There are three distinct sources from which uncertainty arises in any simulation:

First, we have uncertainty inherent to the model you are building. This is a natural process, and if we look at it from a scientific perspective, especially when we introduce quantum mechanics, the presence of subatomic particles is often a probabilistic concept. Following this example, it is easy to create a hypothetical situation, or a theoretical construct, where the assumption is that things will happen in a natural order. However, what if that does not happen?

Take the example of a card game. When you join the table, your assumption or the perception created to confidently bring you to the table is that the dealer will shuffle cards in a random manner. As luck or fate would have it, this is never the case. Every house will always have some tricks up their sleeve. This is the kind of uncertainty that we are talking about. It exists naturally and cannot be wished away. Inherent uncertainty exists by virtue of the presence of certain events.

The second category of uncertainty is incomplete observability. Any system will always seem stochastic especially when we are unable to see all the variables that complete it. It is from the variables that the system derives its unique features. Since you cannot view all the variables, you work with estimates and assumptions, wherein you must factor in probabilities since you do not have 100% certainty of events.

Let's say you participate in a contest where you must choose one of three curtains. Behind each curtain lies a gift. Of the three gifts, two are empty boxes, while one is a suitcase full of money. The outcome that you get is a deterministic output. However, from your perspective, the outcome is not certain.

You have to choose one curtain to get what lies behind it. But by choosing one curtain, you forego whatever lies behind the other two curtains.

The third source of uncertainty is incomplete modeling. In this case, we build or use a model that collects some information and discards it when it is deemed useless. The information that your model discards is the source of uncertainty in the model. What if the discarded information was useful to the model? If you are playing a game of checkers, at the beginning of the game each player has the same number of chances of winning the game. However, when you eliminate some pieces a few moves in, things are not the same anymore. The future position of your pieces is uncertain because you could place each piece anywhere on the board within a cell that you feel it can occupy.

When dealing with probability problems, it is always wise to choose procedures that are simple but uncertain, instead of a certain but complicated one. In machine learning, this concept has been proven over time that in many cases, it is the simple solution that works.

For example, look at the statement "Most people eat." It is relatively easier to build such a program because its explanation is broad, simple and therefore helpful. On the other hand, a statement like "People eat" is very difficult to handle because it includes a lot of exceptions, such as the sick, those who are not hungry, people who are fasting or anyone else who might not be eating for some reason. Building this model will be very expensive because of all the exceptions that must be communicated to the model. This is a model that will have a high susceptibility to failure.

From the beginning when designing a machine learning model, you must remember that uncertainty is part of the development process. Probability theory attempts to provide the relevant solutions we need to build machine learning solutions. This theory was initially constructed to help understand the frequency of occurrences in events, but has since morphed into several aspects of the development process.

Let's look at another example to try and explain the importance of probability theory so far. When diagnosing a patient's illness, doctors use the degree of belief probability. In this case, there is a probability of 1 or 0. 1 represents a diagnosis that the patient does have the illness, while 0 means the patient does not have the illness. This type of probability that is associated directly to the rate at which the said events take place is what we refer to as frequentist probability. In machine learning, this will later form part of an important concept referred to as Bayesian probability.

How does Bayesian probability work in machine learning? First, we list a number of properties that from simple reasoning, we expect to work as a matter of common sense. These are properties that we expect of the uncertainty. From there, we must apply the same rules to the Bayesian probabilities to determine whether the Bayesian and frequentist probabilities are similar.

Let's use the example of choosing a curtain to win whatever prize lies behind that we used earlier. If we calculate the probability that the player will choose one of the three curtains presented given a set of decisionary conditions, we must use the same formula to determine the probability that a patient in a hospital is not infected by some disease based on the symptoms that the patient shows.

Therefore, the use of probability theories in machine learning is to extend the concept of logic into uncertainty, and help us demystify the uncertainty of some events happening. While logic gives us room to use a formal process to determine whether events are true or false, we assume that some propositions must hold for this to work. Probability theory will help us prove whether an additional set of rules can be used to determine the prospect of a given event taking place, in light of other rules applying to the other factors that affect the event.

Random Variables

In probabilistic studies, random variables are variables that can assume any set of values without a specific set of instructions. They are denoted by lower case letters, while the values associated with random variables are assigned lower case script letters. For example, values m_1 and m_2 are possible positions where a random variable M can be true.

If we are working with vectors, the vector variable connotation for the variable M will be expressed as m. A random variable in isolation is used to describe the possible states of an event. To make sense of the position, it is always advisable to use random variables alongside probabilistic distributions, to help us determine the likelihood of an event happening.

When using random variables, you can either have continuous variables or discrete variables. Continuous random variables are described with real values. Discrete random variables, on the other hand, can be defined within finite states. The countability of such variables must not necessarily be assigned to integer values. It is possible to identify them as named states which do not have any integral value attached.

Probabilistic Distribution

In machine learning, probabilistic distribution refers to the likelihood that a given random variable or a set of random variables will assume specific positions. The description of probabilistic distribution will often depend on whether we are dealing with a continuous or discrete variable.

To identify a probabilistic distribution when using discrete variables, you invoke a probability mass function. Generally, probabilistic mass functions are assigned the identifier P. Every random variable must be associated with a unique probability mass function according to the random variable's identity, instead of the name assigned to the function. Therefore, when we use $P(m)$, this is not the same as $P(x)$.

The role of a probability mass function is to establish a condition where we can identify the position of a random variable and the probability of that random variable actually occupying the said position. From this example, the probability of the event M being m can be denoted as $P(m)$, with a probability of 1 telling us that $M = m$ is a certainty, while a probability of 0 telling us that $M = m$ is not possible.

In some cases, these probabilistic explanations might seem ambiguous depending on the nature of data you are working with. To avoid this, it can be expressed as follows:

$$P\ (M = m)$$

In other cases, we will have to define the variable before we use a probabilistic distribution to explain it. In such a scenario, we will have the following:

$$M \sim P(M)$$

When using a probability mass function, take note that this rule can apply to more than one variable. Such a distribution is referred to as a joint probability distribution, and can be expressed as follows:

$$P(M = m, X = x)$$

The function above tells us that $M = m$, and $X = x$, which we can also express as $P(m,x)$. To use a probability mass function on any random variable m, the function P has to meet the following three conditions:

- All the possible positions of m must be defined in the domain of P.
- Any impossible events in the function must have a probability of 0. At the same time, we cannot have any position less than the impossible. In the same reasoning, any event that must happen with certainty must have a probability of 1. If this is true, no other position can assume a greater likelihood of occurrence. These positions can be expressed as follows:

$$\forall m \in m, 0 \leq P(m) \leq 1$$

- We must have a normalized property in the function. In the absence of a normalized property, we can end up with probabilities like $m > 1$, especially when determining the prospect of more than one event happening. The expression for a normalized function is as shown below:

$$\sum_{m \in m} P(m) = 1$$

To explain this further, let's assume a discrete random variable m, with x distribution states. We can establish a uniform distribution on m, which implies that each of the positions possible for this distribution are likely to happen in equal measure. Therefore, the probability mass function for this distribution will be as follows:

$$P(m = m_i) = \frac{1}{x}$$

For all the instances of i, we can determine that all the requirements for a probability mass function are met. Since x is a positive integer, we can also expect the value of $\frac{1}{x}$ to be positive.

Further than that, we can also determine that this is a proper normalized distribution because the following equation holds about the relationship in our function:

$$\sum_i P(m = m_i) = \sum_i \frac{1}{x} = \frac{x}{x} = 1$$

Conditional Probability

As you work on machine learning concepts, you will come across a situation where you need an event to happen assuming that another event has happened. In such a scenario, you have a conditional probability. This scenario can be represented using the format below:

$$m = m \text{ given } n = n \text{ as } P(m = m \mid n = n)$$

Take note that the conditional probability function can never be used on an event that will not happen. Therefore, we can only use and define this condition if the following statement holds:

$$P(m = m) > 0$$

One of the common mistakes that many programmers make is that they struggle to tell the difference between conditional probability with determining the possibility of an event happening if you take a given action. For example, the conditional probability that someone who is born and raised in England speaks English is very high. However, the country of origin never changes if we select a random individual and teach them English. What we perform in this case is an intervention query where we determine the consequence of performing a given action. An intervention query is practically a causal modeling construct, which for the purpose of machine learning, we will not cover in this book. However, you can read on it in your free time because it can be useful in the future.

Conditional Probability Chain Rules

If you are working with data that has several random variables, you can easily determine a joint probability distribution for an independent variable, instead of all the variables in the dataset. To perform such a computation, you will need to learn the product rule for your data, also referred to as the chain rule of probability.

If we have three variables, m, n and c, we will have the following definition function:

$$P(c,m,n) = P(c \mid m,n)P(m,n)$$

$$P(m,n) = P(m \mid n)P(n)$$

$$P(c,m,n) = P(c \mid m,n) \, P(m \mid n)P(n)$$

When you have two variables, m and n, we can refer to them as independent variables if we can express their probability distribution by multiplying any two factors. Of the two factors, one must contain only the variable m, while the other must only contain the variable n. We can represent this in the following manner:

$$\forall m \in m, n \in n, \; p(m = m, n = n) = p(m = m) \; p(n = n)$$

Conditional independence is a situation where we have two variables m and n if we include a random variable x that can factorize for every instance of m and n as shown in the example below:

$$\forall m \in m, n \in n, x \in x, \; p(m = m, n = n | x = x) = p(m = m | x = x) \; p(n = n | x = x)$$

Based on the illustration above, therefore, we can represent independent probabilities and conditional independence according to the relationship between different values.

Covariance, Variance and Expectations

Given a function $f(m)$, an expected value, also referred to as the expectation in relation to the probability distribution $P(m)$, represents the aggregate mean value that is assigned to the f function when we compute the value of m from the probability distribution P.

If we are working with a distribution whose identity is clear from the very beginning, this can be written in terms of the random variable that we expect when the computation is resulted. If we are clear about the position of the random variable, we can eliminate its subscript representation.

When working with linear expectations, you can expect data in the following function format:

$$E_m[\alpha f(m) + \beta g(m)] = \alpha E_m[f(m)] + \beta E_m[g(m)]$$

In the example above, the alpha and beta variables are independent of the variable m.

Variance in a probability distribution tells us the magnitude of the difference between values in our function. We consider the variables in relation to the probabilistic distribution for this assessment. If you result a low variance, the variables are closer to the expected value, and if the variance is high, they are far apart. We can also determine the standard deviation measure for the data, as the square root value of the variance.

In as far as covariance is concerned, we are dealing with a measure of the relationship between any two variables in a probability distribution. Once you compute these estimates, you can use the information to determine the type of relationship between either variables that you will use in your input.

Considering the covariance value, a high absolute return tells us that both of the values you use are so dynamic they keep changing frequently. In fact, at any given point in time, the variables are nowhere close to their relevant averages.

If your covariance value returns a positive integer, this means that both of the variables under scrutiny have very high relative values at the same time. For a negative result, our analysis will reveal that while one of the variables assumes a very low value, the other automatically assumes a very high value. Therefore, the values share an inverse relationship.

We can use correlation computation to normalize the distribution of each variable in the sample data set, so that we can determine only the nature of the relationship between the variables without focusing on the magnitude of the differences between the variables.

From this analysis, therefore, it is evident that dependence and covariance in a probability distribution are related concepts, but they are independent of one another. The relationship exists because either of the two variables we use at input have zero covariance, meaning that they are also independent of each other. Any two variables are considered to be dependent if in the same probabilistic distribution, they both exhibit a non-zero covariance.

If the variables both have zero covariance, then this means that there is no linear relationship between the two. From this assertion therefore, we can determine that in probability distributions, independence carries more weight than zero covariance. The reason for this is because independence does not consider non-linear relationships.

We can also have a situation where two input variables have a zero covariance, but they are dependent on one another.

In information theory, we focus on applied mathematical concepts that determine how much information we can obtain from a given data model. Information theory is used in machine learning to help us understand the relationship between different events. The concept of information theory states that it is highly unlikely that any machine learning will take place when an unlikely event takes place, than when a likely event takes place. We can further quantify this instruction in the following manner:

- Any events that are less likely to occur should be assigned a high information content.
- Any events that are likely to occur should be assigned very low information content. Where necessary, if you are certain that an event will happen, you should not assign it any information content at all.
- Events that are independent of one another should only be assigned additive content.

The statistics and probability concepts that we have outlined in this chapter will play an important role in helping you choose the right inputs and how much weight to assign each input when building a machine learning model. Remember that in machine learning, there is never a guarantee that events will happen as you expect.

Chapter 3: Computations in Machine Learning

One of the most important considerations in machine learning is the demand for a very high numerical computation capacity. What this means is that we need algorithms that can perform mathematical operations to solve complex problems and at the same time, give us an updated solution. The solutions we expect should be delivered by iteration, instead of an analytical procedure that derives the formula as an expression of the solution.

A common example you will come across in machine learning is an optimization problem. In this situation, you determine whether a given argument will maximize or minimize a function in your problem. This is also applicable when solving problems that deal with linear equations.

That being said, however, while it is generally easy to determine the function of a problem using your computer, this can be challenging especially when the function uses real numbers. It is difficult or near impossible to express such numbers without unlimited memory allocation.

Rounding Errors

By definition, the biggest challenge we experience when using computers to solve mathematical problems is that we must find a way to use a finite bit pattern number to represent an unknown value in real numbers. To solve this problem, you will encounter approximation errors in almost all the real number of values you work with. The approximation error is often implemented as a rounding error.

The challenge of using approximation errors in this manner is that when you are rounding off numbers spanning more than one mathematical operation, most of the algorithms that theoretically are correct will fail in application. The reason for this is because the algorithms are not written to accommodate such errors.

An underflow error is one of the common rounding errors that challenge many programmers. Underflow occurs in a situation where you round numbers that are close to zero, to zero. The challenge here is that in most cases, many functions assume a different behavior when their argument is rounded off to zero, instead of a very small but positive integer.

When working on computations, we know from basic math that division by zero results in zero. However, the values we have are not zero, but close to zero. A rounding error will have us performing divisions by zero, the results of which can be catastrophic. We must, therefore, try to avoid this. In some programming environments, such an error will raise an exception, alerting you to check your code.

An overflow error is another common challenge you might encounter. Overflow errors are evident when you round off numbers that are exceptionally large as infinite (∞). If you perform further computations on such a function, the infinite value can return in values that are not numbers, which make it impossible for algorithms to compute.

In Python, you will encounter such problems when using the softmax function. We will illustrate this in an example below.

A softmax function is a common activation function used in Python to convert numbers into probabilities whose aggregate sums to 1. When using the softmax function, you expect the output to be a vector representation of a list of possible outcomes. This is an important factor that aids deep learning models. Let's move on to the illustration.

Say we want to use a softmax function to express the probabilities in a Multinoulli distribution. We will have the function expressed as shown below:

$$softmax(m)_i = \frac{exp(mi)}{\sum exp(mi)}$$

In this example, let's assume a hypothetical situation where m_i is equal to a constant, k. Theoretically, all the outputs will be equal to $\frac{1}{n}$. However, in our math computation, this scenario might not suffice, especially when the value of the constant k, is too large.

In another iteration, if the value of k is negative, then we can expect the result in $exp(k)$ to be an underflow. What this means is that the denominator we use in the softmax function will round off to 0, which leaves us with an undefined final outcome.

In case the value of k is positive and too large, the outcome will be an overflow. Just as we have seen in the case above, we will also have an undefined final outcome. So where does this leave us? To overcome this challenge and avoid problems with the algorithm, we must evaluate the softmax function as shown:

$$softmax(z) \; where \; z = m - max_i \, m_i$$

We will refer to basic algebra to understand the concept above. From algebraic principles, we cannot analytically alter the value of our softmax function by subtracting or adding anything to the vector input. If we subtract $max_i\ m_i$ we end up with the largest possible value to *exp* as zero. Therefore, this will eliminate the risk of having an overflow function. At the same time, we must have at least one item in the denominator with a value of 1. If this is true, this position eliminates the risk of having an underflow in the denominator.

This solves our underflow and overflow problem from a rounding error. However, we are not out of the woods yet. The prospect of an underflow in the numerator might still render our expression a zero function. If we have to impute a *log softmax(z)* by passing the result of a softmax subroutine to a log function, we might end up with an error that results in an infinite result, $-\infty$. To overcome this problem, we create a different function that will determine the *log softmax* using a stable numerical process. To stabilize this log softmax function, we will use the same process we used earlier to stabilize the softmax function above, *softmax(z) where z = m - $max_i\ m_i$.*

Inappropriate Conditioning

When dealing with machine learning algorithms, conditioning is a procedure that outlines how fast you can alter a function in light of subtle changes in the nature of input the model accepts. It is important to understand that most functions will change so fast especially when the input changes slightly. This can cause a problem in computation, especially since such changes often result in rounding errors. As we have discussed in the previous section, rounding errors easily result in erroneous output values.

Let's use the example below to explain inappropriate conditioning:

We have the following function: $f(m) = K^{-1} m$.

If we have the eigenvalue $K \in R^{n \times n}$ representing the function above, the conditioning number will be as follows:

$$max_{ij} \left| \frac{\lambda_j}{\lambda_j} \right|$$

This represents the magnitude ratio of the largest to the smallest eigenvalue. If the value computes a very large result, we end up with a value that is very sensitive to errors at the input. The level of sensitivity depends on the matrix, not the result we get from rounding off values. As a result, if we are working with an inappropriately conditioned matrix, any errors at the input will be compounded.

Most computations used in machine learning algorithms use optimization processes. Optimization basically involves maximizing or minimizing a function $f(m)$ by changing m. An optimization problem can be addressed by minimizing $f(m)$, while a maximization problem can be addressed by minimizing $-f(m)$.

Any underlying function upon which we perform a minimization or maximization operation is referred to as the criterion or the objective function. If we are minimizing a criterion, it can be referred to as an error, a loss or a cost function. In machine learning, values that maximize or minimize functions are assigned a superscript as shown m^*.

Prior knowledge of calculus will come in handy in machine learning, especially when working with optimization algorithms. Let's look at some examples to explain this.

If we have the function, $y = m(x)$, assuming that the values for y and x are real numbers, we can represent this function in a derivative format as shown below:

$$m'(x)$$

This function can also be expressed as follows:

$$\frac{dy}{dx}$$

The derivative $m'(x)$ tells us that if we plot the values on a graph, point x defines the gradient of $m(x)$. From the gradient, we understand what to do to the input values in order to get a proportionate change in the output values. This can be represented as follows:

$$m(x + \varepsilon) \approx m(x) + \varepsilon m'(x)$$

The function we described above will help us in performing minimization tasks because it informs us of what to do to the x variable to get a proportionate change in the y variable. To illustrate this further, we can use the gradient descent procedure.

In the gradient descent, we have already determined that for a reasonably small ε value, $m(x - \varepsilon(f'(m)))$ is less than $m(x)$. To reduce the value of $m(x)$, therefore, we can introduce an opposite value (-) to the derivative.

In case the value of $m'(x)$ is zero, it is impossible for our derivative function to tell us the direction of movement. Such a point in the function is referred to as a stationary or critical point. The point where $m(x)$ is less than all the other points is referred to as the local minimum. At this point, it is not feasible to reduce $m(x)$ any further. On the other hand, the reverse is true for the local maximum. A saddle point is a point in the function where you have neither a maximum or minimum point.

From the illustrations above, we have two types of optimization algorithms used in machine learning. First-order optimization algorithms only use the gradient, while those that use the Hessian matrix are referred to as second-order optimization algorithms.

The Softmax Function

One of the concepts you will engage often in machine learning is the softmax function. This is particularly as you delve deeper into studying deep learning and neural networks. The softmax function is an important part of your learning process in that it helps you convert digital input into a probability distribution. Any probability estimate must always add up to 1.

When using the softmax function, you use vectors that identify the possible distribution you expect of a given list of objects, and their outcome. In machine learning, you will work with classification algorithms from time to time. The softmax function is one of the important features functions that will help you understand how to perform unique operations on such models.

We might not have discussed this function in the earlier books in our series, so for this reason, we will provide an introductory approach, then build on from there to show you how to use this function in Python.

Before you start learning about the softmax function, you must sharpen your knowledge of handling Python lists. Most of the computations you will perform in this operation involve calling data from lists, performing mathematical computations on them, and resulting in an outcome. Therefore, you will use a lot of normalization procedures.

In logistic regression, there are several concepts that you must look at which will help you determine the correct probability of a given distribution. Since we will use the resulting probabilities to determine the target classes in a logistic regression algorithm, we often use the sigmoid function and the softmax function.

The two functions might feature at a similar functionality level, but they have unique differences that set them apart. You, therefore, should know which one to use in any given model for the right output. Of special emphasis is the fact that both of these functions use different mathematical approaches to determine the outcomes. We will look at both of them below, and try to explain the differences and which one you should use depending on the data model you are using.

Comparing Sigmoid and Softmax Functions

In mathematical computations, a sigmoid function can be defined to assume any range of real numbers. In such a function, the possible output values are within the range of 0 - 1. However, in light of reciprocity of conventions, we can also expect figures within the range of -1 to 1.

When plotted on a visual representation, a sigmoid function should return a curve that forms an S shape. If you can recall your statistics classes, you used most of these curves to represent different sets of information. Sigmoid functions must have a cumulative distribution function where the output values are in the range of 0-1.

In statistical analysis, sigmoid functions are commonly used to represent cumulative distribution functions. Let's look at a Python iteration of this function below:

```python
# Install the necessary Python packages

import numpy as np

def sigmoid(inputs):
    """

    Determine the sigmoid for the specified array inputs

    :param inputs:

    :return:
    """

    sigmoid_scores = [1 / float(1 + np.exp(- x)) for x in inputs]

    return sigmoid_scores

sigmoid_inputs = [2, 3, 5, 6]

print "Sigmoid Function Output :: {}".format(sigmoid(sigmoid_inputs))
```

This is a simple example of a sigmoid function implementation. When using this model, it is important to remember that the input values and elements are derived from values present in the list data.

To determine the sigmoid scores for your data, the code snipped *1 / float(1 + np.exp(- x)* is used.

Having seen what a sigmoid function does, we can then compare it with softmax functions. Softmax functions determine the probability distribution of a given number of n events. In simpler terms, when using a softmax model, you will attempt to determine the probability of an event happening over a given number of classes.

One of the benefits of using the softmax function over other functions is the range of possible outputs. Since our output is in the range of 0 - 1, all the probabilities must add up to 1.

When using the softmax function, we compute formulas that derive the exponential parameters for any input data, and the aggregate of the exponentials for all the values that we shall use as inputs. In this case, the softmax function output value is represented by the ratio of the exponential value to the aggregate of exponential values.

Compared to the sigmoid function, the softmax function features probabilities only within the range of 0 and 1. We do not have negative iterations in softmax functions, hence all the values presented must sum up to 1.

This function comes in handy when working with a logistic classification regression model, and can also be used to create neural frameworks depending on the data model expected at every layer. The softmax and sigmoid functions, therefore, are commonly used in deep learning exercises.

The following Python code shows us an example of a softmax function:

```python
# Install the necessary Python package

import numpy as np

def softmax(inputs):
    """

    Determine the softmax for the specific array inputs

    :param inputs:

    :return:
    """

    return np.exp(inputs) / float(sum(np.exp(inputs)))

softmax_inputs = [2, 3, 5, 6]

print "Softmax Function Output :: {}".format(softmax(softmax_inputs))
```

There are two important features that we can use to identify sigmoid functions. First, they always result in a real value output. This is important information that can help you differentiate between this and a softmax function. Secondly, sigmoid functions cannot have a non-positive or non-negative derivative at the beginning of the function. For the purpose of this explanation, a non-positive derivative refers to numbers that are less than or equal to zero, while non-negative derivatives are numbers that are equal to or greater than zero.

From this understanding, we can identify some of the common instances where you will use the sigmoid function from time to time. In a normal logistic regression model, sigmoid functions can be used to perform binary classifications. They can also be used when we use activation functions, especially when building artificial neurons for a computation.

Chapter 4: Machine Learning for Financial Engineering

The magic behind machine learning the world of finance goes beyond the imagination of the average user. However, at this point in time we are more than average users, we are experts and professionals in different aspects of the world of programming. It is in this light that we refute the context of magic. Machine learning is an elaborate process that needs specific prerequisites, namely the correct algorithms, appropriate datasets, and the right infrastructure. With all these in place, you can perform computations in finance that many people would consider magic.

The financial service industry is one where the impact of machine learning has been greatly felt. We interact with these models on a daily basis, and this explains why it is important to discuss it. As an expert in machine learning, there is every chance you might find yourself building a model for a client in the financial services sector, so it is wise to know what you are getting into.

To understand the role of machine learning in finance, we have to look at the definitive approach. Machine learning is essentially teaching computers how to learn without being programmed. Your role is to choose the appropriate model for the task at hand, assign the right data to it, and the model will take it up from there. What the model does is to keep adjusting the variable parameters to ensure that the outcomes are not just right, but keep improving over time. In terms of improvement, you are looking at accuracy, speed of delivery, among other factors important to your objectives in financial modeling.

The financial market is one sector where there exists massive amounts of data. This alone makes it one of the best places to deploy machine learning algorithms. Machine learning needs a lot of data for continuous learning, and the amount of data generated in the financial industry in an hour is unimaginable. It gets even better if you are dealing with datasets that span international markets.

The specific models built for this market will run in the background, releasing results based on the training process. It is wise to train your financial model frequently and keep retraining it on a needs basis to keep it up to date with the happenings in the financial world. Some models are trained daily, others on a weekly basis and so on. The training interval depends on what works for you, and your objectives for building the model.

As a rule of thumb in machine learning, the more data your model has access to, the easier it is for it to deliver accurate results. Thinking of all the petabytes of data in the financial sector, and it is easy to see why this is a good place to deploy machine learning models. Some of the data you can introduce into the model include things like monetary transfers, bills, customer information, and transactions.

The evolution of machine learning and technology in general is still taking shape. We are yet to see the finest form of machine learning in action. However, the fact is that the future of the financial industry and the future of machine learning are intertwined. In as much as this is incredible, there are several companies that still struggle to embrace the value proposition in machine learning for this industry. Some of the reasons why this happens include:

- **Unrealistic expectations**

It is common to come across businesses with largely overrated expectations or unrealistic expectations of the value they hope to derive from machine learning. The fact is that all machine learning models will encounter some form of friction in deployment. With this in mind, therefore, it is wise to take a cautious approach.

When we talk about caution, this means having the right personnel for the job. Companies should bring in someone who is adept at machine learning to become their liaison as the organization shifts to a modern business model. Sadly, such appointments come with cost concerns that most businesses would rather do away with instead of embrace the future of finance.

As a result, the businesses end up with vague demands of what they expect to achieve from implementing machine learning solutions into their businesses. This also makes some businesses shy away from implementing machine learning because they might not have a clear objective of what they hope to achieve.

- **The cost of R&D**

Implementing machine learning models is no easy feat. The cost considerations alone can cripple some companies. These are models that are continuously learning, which also means that at a basic level, the company will have to constantly upgrade their computing resources to sustain the reliability and profitability of implementing the machine learning model in their business.

Other than the cost of implementation, it takes a lot to hire a team that can build a machine model that will fully serve the needs of the business. Many companies outsource this task, but this might have its challenges. A good machine learning model should be built by someone who has intimate understanding of the company, the market, and the industry you operate in. Without this, anything is possible, positive and negative.

- **Lack of expertise**

Now, this is a challenge that does not just affect the financial services sector, but cuts across many other industries, too. We have watched documentaries, attended seminars, and had access to a lot of information about machine learning and how it can improve lives when implemented in strategic positions in many organizations. While this is a good idea, there is a shortage of capable engineers who can take risks and build solutions that address pertinent issues in different environments.

The financial market has for a long time been a preserve for graduates in finance and legal courses. Tech specialists are late entrants into this market, and more importantly, machine learning geniuses. A good number of some of the top financial organizations in the world have programs in place to ensure they can attract some of the best minds in as far as machine learning is concerned.

As businesses in the finance industry adapt to the technological needs of their users and market/industry pressure, the demand is not proportionate to the expertise available in the market. With this in mind, many of the top machine learning experts operate on a contractual project-to-project basis. As the demand keeps growing, however, we will see an influx of programmers getting absorbed into the financial industry, so this problem might not persist for so long.

Importance of Machine Learning in Finance

Having looked at some of the challenges that companies experience in terms of deploying and integrating machine learning into their businesses, why is it important to take advantage of such technology? What makes machine learning a valid discussion that companies cannot take for granted anymore?

- **Process automation**

There are several tasks in a financial environment that do not have to be carried out all the time. These are tasks that can be automated to improve efficiency. Something as simple as a ticketing system has eliminated unnecessary lines in many banking halls. Instead, customers simply walk in, get a ticket number, and head to the lounge and wait their turn. However, this is a very simple explanation. There are many other complex challenges that can be automated through machine learning and improve the experience of customers and businesses, in the process reducing the cost of operation.

- **The case for productivity**

Each business needs employees to be at their productive optimum if they are to help the business realize its financial goals. This is one area where machine learning can come in handy. Machine learning models can be implemented to help improve the user experiences. This can further be translated into increased productivity and increased revenue streams at the end of the financial trading period.

- **The security approach**

The financial sector is always a prime target for attacks. Successful attempts fleece customers billions in aggregate losses, and the trickle-down effect of such losses can be felt when companies are forced to downsize or reconsider their future in the industry. Machine learning has helped many organizations implement security features that do not just protect the customer, but ensure the business is also shielded from unnecessary risk. This, coupled with compliance regulations, helps businesses meet their needs and stay competitive.

In as far as financial data and the industry is concerned, there are many machine learning algorithms available, most of which are open-source projects. Therefore, there is no reason why companies should shy away from embracing machine learning. Besides, those companies that have a sizeable financial allocation can even invest further in the industry and build some of the finest machine learning models the world has ever seen.

Machine Learning Applications in Finance

For all the talk about machine learning in finance, where are these models already implemented, such that companies that are lagging behind can find something to learn from?

- **Automated processes**

Of all the machine learning deployments in the world of finance, process automation is one of the most important and prevalent. Many repetitive manual tasks have been replaced, thereby increasing productivity in the companies where the deployment happened.

What does this mean for the organizations? It allows them the chance to optimize their expenditure, scale up service provision, and more importantly, ensure that their customers have a good experience with their services. Some common process automation processes in machine learning in the financial sector include using chatbots, automated paperwork, automated call centers, and using game theory for training employees.

How are companies doing this? Let's look at some real examples of machine learning in the financial sector.

JPMorgan Chase probably has one of the most referenced machine learning systems in the financial world. The Contract Intelligence model is primarily a natural language processing machine learning model. Through this, they managed to sort legal documents accordingly, in the process, obtaining important information from the documents. How useful has this model been to the company? Before implementation, such processes would consume more than 350,000 hours. Through machine learning, they managed to reduce this to a few hours, in the process saving the company time and labor hours.

Apart from JPMorgan Chase, the Bank of New York Mellon Corporation also successfully deployed machine learning into their business processes, helping them to achieve annual savings worth $300,000. Other than that, this implementation further helped the company make several improvements in operations.

In Ukraine, Privatbank successfully deployed chatbot assistants to their web and mobile platforms. These chatbots have since helped the bank increase their engagement rate with customers by helping them resolve issues faster. Through this process, the bank eventually reduced reliance on assistants, and experienced increased customer satisfaction.

- **Security consideration**

The world of finance is not new to security threats. In fact, this is usually the prime target for many attacks. Given the increase in transaction volume and transaction data worldwide, security has become an important subject today. Many third-party applications are currently in use, all of which collect any kind of information that the owners find appropriate.

Fraudulent activities have been on the rise given the rate at which tech companies are expanding, and customers are getting connected to devices online. The proliferation of technology and ease of use of networks is not just limited to customers and businesses. Even hackers enjoy a good internet connection and the benefit of using some of the top brains in the business.

Machine learning has enabled financial organizations to identify fraudulent activities faster than before. Many banks today actively monitor all transactions that run through their servers. They run algorithms that monitor accounts and the associated card information. If they identify any information that is uncharacteristic of the account holder, such accounts are flagged for further review. This process has helped many banks stop fraudulent attacks on their customers right in their tracks.

In most cases these machine learning models request further identification or any other relevant information before the transaction can be validated. If there is sufficient evidence to prove that the transaction is fraudulent, the model would block the transaction instantly. Therefore, through machine learning, banks have managed to up their game in as far as preventing fraud is concerned.

While still on security, machine learning is also used in financial monitoring. This is a procedure where experts at the bank monitor specific micropayments that might be part of a money laundering ring. One of the techniques common in money laundering that can be detected by machine learning is smurfing.

Machine learning models have also helped to boost network security in the industry. Systems are specifically trained to identify network threats and act on them immediately. Since the systems monitor and process thousands of activities at the same time, they can identify threats in a very short time, and act on them accordingly. Some of the top companies that have heavily invested in machine learning include PayPay, Skrill, and Payoneer.

- **Credit scores**

Insurance and financial engineers interact with machine learning models all the time. This often takes place when underwriting insurance policies or determining credit scores. Machine learning models are trained to monitor thousands of customer profiles based on different kinds of data entry. Once the system is properly trained, it can analyze customer data and assign credit scores according to the customer's characteristics and performance history.

If you look at the size of historical data on consumers held by banks and insurance companies, there is a lot of value in that data that can help to train machine learning models. Today, many financial organizations have gone a notch higher and leveraged their datasets against the information held by utility companies. This means that they can use your utility bills to help determine your credit scores.

- **Trading in financial markets**

Personally, many people struggle to make astute financial decisions. When they get to the financial markets, it is even worse. From beginner traders to expert traders, an element of greed usually steps in and overshadows the trader's consciousness. Through machine learning, you can implement algorithmic trading to help you make astute decisions in the financial market.

How do these models work? Generally, they monitor financial news and identify patterns that might result from events in the news. This way, they can predict accurately whether prices will fall or increase. Based on this information, the model can either purchase, sell, or hold onto your stocks if you set it to do so.

These algorithms are built to monitor thousands of databases and data sources at the same time, something that would be impossible for any individual to do on their own. Based on this performance, these algorithms allow you an edge in performance against the market average. If your trading position is better than the market average, you can make quite a fortune online.

- **Advisory services**

One of the emerging trends in the financial industry is the use of robo-advisors. These advisors are actively implemented either as recommendations or in portfolio management. In the case of recommendations, we have seen several uses of this practice not just in the financial sector, but also in the retail sector. The advisors study customer data to determine appropriate products that are suitable for your needs and recommend them. Most of the time customers prefer robo-advisors over personal finance advisors because the cost is lower, and there is no chance of personal bias influencing their decisions.

In as far as portfolio management is concerned, machine learning algorithms are used to manage client assets online. When using such a model, you provide information about your financial goals and assets, then the advisor automatically allocates your assets to specific investment vehicles depending on your risk profile, and more importantly, your financial goals.

In the past, many people have suffered at the hands of financial advisors who made personal decisions from their accounts. Some have been paid back, others are still in court. However, the fact remains that the missed investment opportunities will never be earned back.

On the part of businesses, this also allows them to reduce the risk of malpractice by their employees. Instead of taking a personal interest in a customer's portfolio, the customer is in full control and decides what they want to do through the robo-advisory services.

- **Risk management**

Many financial institutions have implemented machine learning solutions in their risk business, and for a good reason. It is not always easy to determine the risk profile of an investment or a client at par. Businesses exist to maximize their potential returns, and this is one of the reasons why they have to take extra measures to ensure they put their money in the right investment vehicles.

There have been approaches to studying risk profiles for different investments in the past, but these have always had their challenges. To overcome this, companies are currently investing in machine learning technologies that can help them identify risky portfolios based on the current market trends and patterns, and from there, they can act accordingly. This way, they can use the information and technology at their disposal to benefit from a potentially hazardous situation, or avert a crisis.

This concept is not only limited to portfolios. Financial institutions must also look at the ease with which they can predict crisis situations in the market. The financial crisis in 2018 caught a lot of financial institutions unawares, and as a result many businesses closed. Given the nature of machine learning techniques available at the moment, a repeat of such an experience might not really affect many businesses directly, especially those that have predictive measures in place. They should be able to create a buffer to protect them from such challenges.

- **Improved customer services**

One of the challenges that many businesses have in the financial sector is the inability to serve the needs of the customer effectively. In the money business, when corporates are making a lot of money, it is easy to overlook the importance of the small customer. Most companies simply focus on their core business areas and their biggest clients, while the smaller clients suffer.

Poor customer service has dogged the industry for years, and it is no secret that this can be resolved very easily through machine learning. Many companies that have implemented some innovative machine learning models have managed to cater to their customers better, and experienced an improved customer service rating. There are many tools that can be used for this service. Chatbots, for example, have been a welcome addition in the course of doing business. Customers can interact with these bots and get answers to their concerns without having to go to the company, or spend on their phone bills calling into the company for assistance. Most of such calls usually end up with the customer on hold for a long time as the customer service representative tries to find a solution. All this can be avoided through machine learning.

- **Efficient management practices**

The role of digital assistants in the modern workplace is so important that many companies are increasingly adopting these techniques. Digital assistants help to increase functionality, effectiveness, and efficiency of service provision by taking away the burden of performing mundane tasks. Instead, the executives focus on working on their core business functions.

There are many digital assistant models available in the market at the moment. All these models are built with specific needs in mind. It is advisable that before you choose a model, you make sure your needs align with the model you select. This is important if you are not building the model from scratch, and instead choose to outsource support from external sources.

Companies that have the necessary skills in a dev department can enjoy better performance since the developers already understand what the company is about, and the needs that the machine learning model should address.

These models are built to learn different behavioral traits of each user, and model their interaction based on the responses that they receive on a regular basis. With time, they can make accurate predictions for the user.

- **Marketing**

Machine learning has been extensively implemented in the marketing department for many organizations for a long time. The marketing department anchors other departments, especially the finance department. Machine learning models can be deployed in this segment to help in making important predictions based on company performance and responses from customers.

Predictions in the marketing department are a construct of historical data on different behavior patterns, either of users or the executives in the company. Executives in the marketing department can tell how performances were affected in the past based on specific actions or activities they initiated to promote some products. This forms a learning point, such that they know what to tweak in their activities in order to replicate previous performance results, or what to change to improve on past experiences.

When interacting with customers, a predictive model is a useful tool in that it will help determine the best approach to engage customers. Many models used in the marketing industry will look at things like the customer's browsing history, their frequent activity online, and any other relevant data about the customer that is available. This way, it is easier to recommend suitable products to the customer without risking backlash.

Given that many financial institutions are increasingly adopting machine learning models in marketing, we can expect that there will be more innovation in this sector in the coming years, which translates to better predictive models, and a boost to the marketing department in as far as meeting their strategic objectives is concerned.

- **Interpreting documents**

Document interpretation is an important aspect of machine learning that financial organizations are coming to terms with. The legal arm of financial organizations usually handle a lot of documents, most of which must be interpreted and used urgently. Some businesses outsource some of these tasks. However, the challenge with outsourcing is that in most cases, the quality is not as good as the intended use demands. Therefore, the company has to spend more on time and resources to analyze such documents properly and use them as they intend to.

Companies that cannot outsource their documents must spend on more skilled employees to handle the interpretation processes. The JP Morgan Chase example mentioned earlier is a good example of how companies can benefit from machine learning concepts like natural language processing. Work that should take thousands of hours can now be processed in minutes.

- **Content creation**

The content creation industry is not far behind in as far as the benefits of machine learning in the financial world are concerned. Machine learning has yielded some important models that have made work easier for many users who curate content, especially in the financial sector. Content creators no longer have to sit down for hours and write their financial analysis, proofread the content, and pass it on to their editors.

Instead, they can use different machine learning models specifically built to help users overcome the challenges involved in writing lengthy posts. You can simply speak into a model that will transcribe everything you say. From the output, you can proofread once to identify any errors or incongruence of ideas before you push the content online. This is one of the disruptive features of natural language processing that we will experience more over the next few years.

The good thing about machine learning is that models are increasingly improving in their capacity to understand our communication cues. With time, the model will learn and accurately interpret different language dialects as we have seen in Google Translate over the years. Therefore, instead of spending a long time writing your financial summary, or preparing stock reports, you can use machine learning algorithms to handle that with ease.

- **Settling trade agreements**

A trade settlement is a procedure where you exchange some payment for a security instrument in the form of a trade on the stock market. While we have made significant strides over the years in as far as electronic transactions are concerned, settling trade agreements is still not possible as instantaneously as most people would wish. There are many issues that prevent this from becoming a reality.

Many of the modern platforms where clients can trade have tried implementing some machine learning algorithms to help them overcome most of the challenges experienced in completing trades. However, if we look at the large trade volumes expected in such platforms, most of the programs used to handle such settlements will always struggle at some point. It gets worse in entities that still use manual processes to resolve settlements, especially those that have failed.

Machine learning algorithms can help overcome this challenge by identifying simple patterns associated with successful or failed trades. Since this can be done in a very short time, users can easily expect to conduct and complete their trades in seconds. Since it is possible from consistent training to identify the probability of some trades failing, the machine learning model can then make accurate predictions and use this information to speed up processes both for the user and the trading platform.

- **Custom solutions to custom problems**

Given that many organizations are embracing machine learning models, it is obvious that machine learning will become the hottest topic in the financial world in the near future, if it is not already. Currently, many organizations are building applications that can solve simple problems for them. It is understandable that implementing a fully fledged machine learning model will have its challenges in as far as adoption is concerned. This is also why many organizations are reluctant to implement such systems.

A lot of companies use outsourced models. In the face of competition, there comes a time when outsourced models are insufficient, because competitors who use the same model can easily predict your outcomes based on previous performance history. Therefore, we will see a trend where many companies invest in serious development teams that can study their operations, understand them, and build models that can address their needs accordingly.

Currently, we see tech giants like Google and IBM investing heavily into machine learning technologies, and many other companies will follow suit. The end result is to create models that are easy to use, powerful, and highly accurate at predictive analytics. Since there is no one-size-fits-all approach to machine learning, there is a lot of room for research and development in this field. The financial industry is one of the best for deploying machine learning models given the amount of data available. We will definitely see more activity in this industry, especially if we factor in developments like decentralization as we can see in the world of cryptocurrency.

Implementing Machine Learning in Finance

Given all that we have discussed about machine learning in finance, you'd be surprised that the uptake is not so promising. Even companies that have sound financial backing are yet to embrace machine learning fully. There is a lot of value in this technology that should be implemented in financial circles for the benefit of businesses and customers alike, and more importantly, for the greater benefit of the industry.

One of the challenges inherent in the industry is implementation. Inappropriate KPIs in business have affected many organizations, holding them back. As a result, those who implement machine learning end up missing their targets, and waste a lot of money in the process. Besides, just because you have the right infrastructure for machine learning does not mean it will be a success for your project.

Having the infrastructure in place is important, complete with all the necessary resources. Beyond that, however, you must ensure you have the expertise, and sustainable environment that will help you realize the true potential of machine learning working for your company.

The moment you realize and understand the importance of machine learning in your business and how it will help you get closer to your business objectives, it is easier to work on suitable and appropriate KPIs that will deliver realistic returns on your investment. The following are guidelines that will help you implement machine learning in a financial environment:

First, make sure you have access to the necessary data streams. Without data, scalable data to be precise, your machine learning model is useless. It should not buckle under the weight of additional or updated data because generally, it is built to consume more data as time goes.

The adoption process is the next step in implementation. Before adopting any machine learning model, make sure you consider the conditions unique to your business. There are many ways you can adopt a model without affecting your end result negatively.

At adoption, it is wise not to complicate matters. The simplest solution that delivers results is usually a good idea. Many companies make the mistake of going for a complex model, under the guise that sophistication will give them a competitive advantage over their peers. However, this never ends well. Sophistication must be matched by the right resources.

Chapter 5: Machine Learning for Spam Filtration

Ever taken time to think about the psychology of spam mails? Spam mails are in many cases a psychological game of wits. Think about it for a moment. Spammers actively preys on the recipient's greed by trapping them with an illusion. Woe unto them if they fall for it. What other explanation would suffice for you to imagine a Prince in an unheard of kingdom in a country where no one you know has ever visited, would ask you to move to their country? Or a war hero who has amassed an insane amount of wealth but cannot access it? So for some reason, the war hero reaches out to you out of the blue and needs you to send them some money to process their finances, then they can share a slice of their fortune with you.

These sound like folklore, but rest assured that a lot of people fall for such scams online. I first came across such scams almost 20 years ago just before joining high school. The fact that these scams are still perpetuated today means that many people have been victims and it is a thriving enterprise.

Email service providers have been actively working to protect their clients from such frauds for years. How do they manage to filter spam from legitimate mail? Where does machine learning come in?

To filter spam from your emails, the providers use a classifier known as the Naive Bayes classifier. This is an algorithm that operates on the Bayes Classification rule. Generally, what the algorithm does is to isolate and study all features in emails sent to you. By looking at the features in isolation, the algorithm can give many probabilities for a single feature under consideration.

Having studied the features in isolation, the algorithm then aggregates all the features to deliver the final outcome, which is the ultimate probability. These calculations are performed for as many classes as can be deduced from the data available. At the end of the analysis, the class that has the greatest probability becomes the ultimate determinant.

Applying Bayes Rule

In the case of spam filters, the email sent to you is the object of interest. The features that the machine learning algorithm will look at are unique keywords present in the email. The algorithm then flags specific keywords that have been used in spam mails before. Remember that the model also maintains a database of other keywords used in spam mails collected over time, therefore you end up with an elaborate database of spam keywords from which decisions can be made.

From the Bayes rule, a simple formula for filtering spam should look like this:

P(SPAM / Word) = [P (Word / SPAM) x] x P(SPAM) / P(Word)

P(Word) = P(Word/SPAM) x P(SPAM) + P(Word/ Not Spam) x P(Not Spam)

While the spam filtration process might seem like one of the most difficult tasks, it is actually one of the easiest machine learning tasks to build and implement. First, you must ensure you have a dataset that contains emails.

To help you understand the process even better, prior knowledge of natural language processing might come in handy for you. In the procedure we will highlight below, we will use the publicly available Enron dataset.

Once you have the data, the first step is to print all the files and directories that you will use going forward.

Create a spam training folder on your computer and name it *Enron Spam*. You will also need to learn more about the layout of emails, so try and refresh your memory on this before you proceed.

We will be working with two classes of emails, spam mail and clean mail, for legitimate emails. You should have the following data:

rootdir = "C:\\Users\\User\\Downloads\\Data Sources\\Enron Spam"

for directories, subdirs, files in os.walk(rootdir):

   print(directories, subdirs, len(files))

C:\Users\User\Downloads\Data Sources\Enron Spam ['enron1', 'enron2', 'enron3', 'enron4', 'enron5', 'enron6'] 0

C:\Users\User\Downloads\Data Sources\Enron Spam\enron1 ['clean', 'spam'] 1

C:\Users\User\Downloads\Data Sources\Enron Spam\enron1\clean [] 3272

C:\Users\User\Downloads\Data   Sources\Enron Spam\enron1\spam [] 1200

C:\Users\User\Downloads\Data   Sources\Enron Spam\enron2 ['clean', 'spam'] 1

The next procedure is to print files in the spam folder and the clean folder. There are several files that are contained in these folders. Instead of printing them all, you will only focus on the two folders that we need. To make your work easier, you can use the *os.path.split()* to determine the directory you are currently working from. This should give you the following output:

print(os.path.split("C:\\Users\\User\\Downloads\\Data Sources\\Enron Spam\\enron1\\clean"))

print(os.path.split("C:\\Users\\User\\Downloads\\Data Sources\\Enron Spam\\enron1\\clean")[0])

print(os.path.split("C:\\Users\\User\\Downloads\\Data Sources\\Enron Spam\\enron1\\clean")[1])

('C:\\Users\\User\\Downloads\\Data   Sources\\Enron Spam\\enron1', 'clean')

C:\Users\User\Downloads\Data   Sources\Enron Spam\enron1

Ham

The next step is to manipulate the code to ensure that you are working on the correct folder. The procedure is similar to the procedure in the step above, only that in this case, you are printing only the spam and clean folders.

for directories, subdirs, files in os.walk(rootdir):

```
if (os.path.split(directories)[1] == 'clean'):

    print(directories, subdirs, len(files))
```

#This section shows you whether you are working on the correct folder or not

```
if (os.path.split(directories)[1] == 'spam'):

    print(directories, subdirs, len(files))

directories, subdirs, len(files))
```

C:\Users\User\Downloads\Data   Sources\Enron Spam\enron1\clean [] 3272

C:\Users\User\Downloads\Data   Sources\Enron Spam\enron1\spam [] 1200

C:\Users\User\Downloads\Data   Sources\Enron Spam\enron2\clean [] 4261

C:\Users\User\Downloads\Data   Sources\Enron Spam\enron2\spam [] 1296

Why is it important to make sure you are working on the correct folder? The code snippet

```
if (os.path.split(directories)[1] == 'clean'):

    print(directories, subdirs, len(files))
```

helps you ensure that when you are ready to read the files, only two folders are affected, the spam and clean folders. This way, you work is neat and clean, and there is very little room for error.

Once you are certain you are using the correct folders, you need to derive data from the spam list and the clean list.

We shall take a closer look at the code now to identify something different.

for directories, subdirs, files in os.walk(rootdir):

    if (os.path.split(directories)[1] == 'clean'):

      for filename in files:

        with open(os.path.join(directories, filename)) as f:

        data = f.read()

        clean_list.append(data)

The identifier code has not changed, except that we have introduced the segment below:

    for filename in files:

      with open(os.path.join(directories, filename)) as f:

      data = f.read()

      clean_list.append(data)

For the section above, the next step is to create a loop, open each of the files, read the messages and add them to the spam and clean list respectively as shown below:

    if (os.path.split(directories)[1] == 'spam'):

      for filename in files:

        with open(os.path.join(directories, filename)) as f:

        data = f.read()

        spam_list.append(data)

Your code should run well. If that is not the case, you will probably have a Unicode error. With this error, check all the files that are flagging errors using your preferred text editor. Most probably, the affected files do not contain pure text messages. Special characters in the message probably mean this is spam.

The next phase is to introduce the Naive Bayes algorithm into your data. This should help you identify spam from normal mail. This algorithm has specific requirements for input format. We will approach this in the following manner:

create a function that must be passed in words to return a dictionary form as follows

{Word1: True, Wordn: True}

You can do away with stop words

def create_word_features(words):

   Pass

We will first write the function *create_word_features()* and then use it in the algorithm as shown:

clean_list = []

spam_list = []

The process is the same, with a few changes as shown below

1.Use *word_tokenize* to break down the sentences

2. Introduce the *create_word_features()* function

       print(clean_list[0])

       print(spam_list[0])

Using the new function created, you should have the following sample code:

```
def create_word_features(words):

    my_dict = dict( [ (word, True) for word in words] )

    return my_dict

create_word_features(["the", "slow", "black", "quick", "a", "jackal"])

{'a': True, black: True, "jackal": True, "slow": True, 'the': True}
```

In the example above, we are building a dictionary that returns True for all words. We are not eliminating any stop words so far.

Using the function created earlier, we will then use the previous code as shown below:

```
for directories, subdirs, files in os.walk(rootdir):

    if (os.path.split(directories)[1] == 'clean'):

        for filename in files:

            with        open(os.path.join(directories, filename)) as f:

                data = f.read()

                clean_list.append(data)
```

At this juncture, what we have instructed the machine to do is to read the data and add it to the clean list. In so doing, the new list should look like this:

with open(os.path.join(directories, filename), encoding="latin-1") as f:

    data = f.read()

    # We are reading a large stream of data, so it is safer to decongest it into words.

    words = word_tokenize(data)

    clean_list.append((create_word_features(words), "clean"))

The function *words = word_tokenize(data)* helps us decongest the data in the code above into manageable bits.

When that is done, we can then call the function as shown:

    clean_list.append((create_word_features(words), "clean"))

Why do we have *clean* at the end of the function? This is to remind the algorithm that the text contained in this function is of the type clean. Therefore, the machine does not care about the nature of the word, all that matters is whether it is consistent with the specific classification. We shall repeat the process for the spam list too as shown below:

clean_list = []

spam_list = []

 # The process is similar, with a few changes as shown:

 # 1.Use word_tokenize to break down the sentences

 # 2. Introduce the create_word_features() function

for directories, subdirs, files in os.walk(rootdir):

```
if (os.path.split(directories)[1] == 'clean'):

    for filename in files:

        with    open(os.path.join(directories,    filename),
encoding="latin-1") as f:

            data = f.read()

            # We are reading a large stream of data, so it is
safer to decongest it into words.

            clean_list.append((create_word_features(words),
"clean"))

    if (os.path.split(directories)[1] == 'spam'):

    for filename in files:

        with    open(os.path.join(directories,    filename),
encoding="latin-1") as f:

            data = f.read()

            # We are reading a large stream of data, so it is
safer to decongest it into words.

            spam_list.append((create_word_features(words),
"spam"))

print(clean_list[0])

print(spam_list[0])
```

Looking at the code above, it seems a bit complicated. However, if you follow the explanation before it, you will realize that it is a simple process, just split into two parts, one for the clean list and another for the spam list.

Next, we need to build training and testing data to call the Naive Bayes filter. We will use the code below to join our clean list and spam list filters then randomize the data as shown:

clean_list = []

spam_list = []

 # The process is similar, with a few changes as shown:

 # 1.Use word_tokenize to break down the sentences

 # 2. Introduce the create_word_features() function

for directories, subdirs, files in os.walk(rootdir):

  if (os.path.split(directories)[1] == 'clean'):

    for filename in files:

      with   open(os.path.join(directories,   filename), encoding="latin-1") as f:

        data = f.read()

        # We are reading a large stream of data, so it is safer to decongest it into words.

        clean_list.append((create_word_features(words), "clean"))

  if (os.path.split(directories)[1] == 'spam'):

    for filename in files:

      with   open(os.path.join(directories,   filename), encoding="latin-1") as f:

data = f.read()

 # We are reading a large stream of data, so it is safer to decongest it into words.

spam_list.append((create_word_features(words), "spam"))

print(clean_list[0])

print(spam_list[0])

combined_list = clean_list + spam_list

random.shuffle(combined_list)

After that, we must assign the data into categories for training and testing accordingly. Say we are using a 70:30 ratio for training and test data respectively, we will have the following:

 # Build a test and train group

 # 70% of data is for training. 30% of data is for test

Once we have this classification, the next step is to introduce the algorithm filter for accuracy as shown:

 # Introduce the Naive Bayes filter

 # Use the test data to determine the accuracy

*print("Accuracy is: ", accuracy * 100)*

With this information, the next step is to determine the training data as shown:

*training_part = int(len(combined_list) * .7)*

We have converted from percentages to *int()* so that we work with whole numbers. From there, we can then classify the data into training and test data as shown:

```
print(len(combined_list))

training_set = combined_list[:training_part]

test_set = combined_list[training_part:]

print (len(training_set))

print (len(test_set))

43717

33601

10116
```

Based on this training and test data, we can use the Naive Bayes filter as shown below:

```
# Introduce the Naive Bayes filter

classifier                          =
NaiveBayesClassifier.train(training_set)

# determine accuracy, using the test data

accuracy = nltk.classify.util.accuracy(classifier, test_set)

print("Accuracy is: ", accuracy * 100)

Accuracy is:  98.5071
```

A 98.5071% accuracy is a commendable rating for our model. The following are some other important details that we derived from the dataset:

classifier.show_most_informative_features(20)

enron = True	clean : spam	=	3688.6 : 1.0
cron = True	clean : spam	=	567.0 : 1.0
php = True	spam : clean	=	406.2 : 1.0
713 = True	clean : spam	=	316.3 : 1.0
louise = True	clean : spam	=	289.2 : 1.0
xls = True	clean : spam	=	271.8 : 1.0
harvey = True	clean : spam	=	257.4 : 1.0
briggs = True	clean : spam	=	241.5 : 1.0
ect = True	clean : spam	=	221.2 : 1.0
scheduling = True	clean : spam	=	199.6 : 1.0
= True	clean : spam	=	174.1 : 1.0
sex = True	spam : clean	=	172.3 : 1.0
hemp = True	clean : spam	=	158.7 : 1.0
1923 = True	spam : clean	=	142.1 : 1.0
spam = True	spam : clean	=	135.1 : 1.0
parsing = True	clean : spam	=	127.6 : 1.0
penis = True	spam : clean	=	107.2 : 1.0

From the data above, we can tell that it is highly likely we will encounter the keyword *Enron* in clean mail rather than spam. On the other hand, you can also tell that *php* and *sex* are more likely to show up in spam than clean mail.

So, from this process, how do we determine whether an email is spam or clean? Let's look at the example below, where we have three emails we need to categorize accordingly:

Determine whether the mail is spam or clean mail

1. Use word_tokenzise

2. create_word_features

3. Use the classify function

First email

> '"Howdy th ere sex king :-)
>
> I relish your c0ck asap... my husband is away on a business trip. .))
>
> My screen id is Barmby.
>
> Here is my account: http:nxgatxbnd.SexyBadoo.ru
>
> Waiting for u!'"

Second email

> '"To appreciate you as one of our best customers, we are offering 20% OFF your next purchase from our online store www.onlinestore.com. To claim this offer, use the promotional code, BEST20 at checkout. This code can only be used once for each customer. Enjoy fast and free shipping on all books within our store.
>
> We also have hundreds of thousands of books available at up to 80% off the retail price and

add more books to our collection daily. Check our listings regularly for new additions."

Third email

'"I recently completed the production and uploaded 4 new videos in the tutorials section. In this section, I will show you how to analyze a dataset with millions of files step-by-step in a half an hour of video recordings.

I have also created source code that free and premium users can access so that everyone using my tutorial is working on the same platform. "

We can clearly tell the first email is spam. The second email is also spam, but has not been worded to explicitly suggest it is spam. The third email however, is a legitimate email and should not be flagged as spam.

If you follow the instructions outlined as we have discussed, you should have the following:

words = word_tokenize(mail_1)

features = create_word_features(words)

print("Mail 1 is :" ,classifier.classify(features))

Mail 1 is : spam

words = word_tokenize(mail_2)

features = create_word_features(words)

print("Mail 2 is :" ,classifier.classify(features))

words = word_tokenize(mail_2)

features = create_word_features(words)

```
print("Mail 2 is :" ,classifier.classify(features))

Mail 2 is : spam

words = word_tokenize(mail_3)

features = create_word_features(words)

print("Mail 3 is :" ,classifier.classify(features))

Mail 3 is : clean
```

As you can see, something that looks so complicated can actually be a simple process, if only you take time and break it down into manageable chunks. Remember that with spam filters, the nature of content keeps evolving, so you must also use training and test data that has evolved to capture the content you are trying to filter.

Chapter 6: Machine Learning for Sentiment Analysis

Sentiments mean so much to different people. In the modern world, sentiments hold much value in different disciplines. We have seen this particularly in business and politics, hence explaining why the active players in these industries are always keen on recommendations, reviews, opinions, age, and anything else that can give them an idea of what people think about them.

Sentiments are not just limited to these entities though, because even at personal level, you are often interested in learning what people think about you. This is why when you receive notifications on your social media apps, the first notifications you check are those where your account handle is tagged, then you can check the others later.

Advances in technology have made it easier for us to analyze data in the most efficient manner. Sentiment analysis is one of the most important elements of natural language processing (NLP) that machine learning models use to determine the polarity of documents and group them accordingly. The polarity of a document basically means that machines try to read the attitude of the author in the document. Sentiment analysis is also referred to as opinion mining.

One of the important assignments you will perform in sentiment analysis is to group documents according to emotions and opinions of the authors on the subject. To highlight important steps and processes in sentiment analysis, we will attempt to review a movie dataset from IMDb.

IMDb is one of the largest opinion databases for movies known today. In this database, users review movies they have watched, and their opinions are either positive or negative. A positive rating on IMDb is a review of at least six stars, while a negative rating is a review of less than five stars. In our examples in the coming sections, we will look at how we can obtain useful information from these reviews, and create a machine learning model that can tell us what reviewers think of the movie. The movie review dataset we will use is available here. It should be around 80MB in size.

Once you obtain the dataset, the next step is to obtain individual files from the database. For this task we will use Pandas *DataFrame* objects. Be patient as this file is loaded into your system. Depending on your computing resources, the procedure should take no more than 10 minutes.

A Python good package that can help you visualize progress in this project is the Python Progress Indicator (PyPrind). To install it, use the following commands:

```
pip install pyprind

>>> import pyprind

    >>> import pandas as pd

    >>> import os

    >>> pbar = pyprind.ProgBar(50000)

    >>> labels = {'pos':1, 'neg':0}

    >>> df = pd.DataFrame()
```

```
>>> for s in ('test', 'train'):

... ... ...

for l in ('pos', 'neg'):

  path ='./aclImdb/%s/%s' % (s, l)

  for file in os.listdir(path):

...          with open(os.path.join(path, file), 'r') as
infile:...

  txt = infile.read()

...                df = df.append([[txt, labels[l]]],
ignore_index=True)

...          pbar.update()

>>> df.columns = ['review', 'sentiment']

0%                   100%

[#############################] |
ETA[sec]: 0.000

Total time elapsed: 822.061 sec
```

As you work on this code, take note that you are reading around 50,000 documents from the database. We have used the *for* loops to specify the testing and training documents within the *aclImdb* directory.

This dataset already has the class labels identified and sorted accordingly, so our next procedure will be shuffling the data frame to create the training and testing models using the *permutation* function. To make work easier, we will save our work in a CSV file as shown below:

```
>>> import numpy as np

>>> np.random.seed(0)

>>> df = df.reindex(np.random.permutation(df.index))

>>> df.to_csv('./movie_data.csv', index=False)
```

Make sure you save the document correctly because you will call on it several times. You should be able to see a few samples of the dataset in your notebook.

An important Python procedure that we will use is converting category data like words and text into numerical data. This makes it easier to pass such information into your machine learning model. To do this, you will use the *bag of words* model. This model uses numerical vector features to represent text data.

To use the *bag of words* model, we will first build a vocabulary that contains unique tokens. The tokens in our case are words that are used in the documents we analyze. Once we create the dictionary, the next step is to build a vector from every document we analyze. This vector should tell us how many times a given word is used in each document.

Remember that the unique words used in every document only represent a small fraction of all the words we will introduce in the *bag of words* model. Therefore, most of the time, feature vectors contain zeros.

Word Transformation

We will use the *bag of words* model to build a dictionary from each of the documents we access in this database. Using Scikit-Learn, we will use the CountVectorizer class for this. Through this class, we can convert a text data array into the *bag of words* model we need as shown below:

```
>>> import numpy as np

>>> from sklearn.feature_extraction.text import CountVectorizer

>>> count = CountVectorizer()

>>> docs = np.array([
...     'The weather is amazing',
...     'The wind is calm',
...     'The weather is amazing and the wind is calm'])

>>> bag = count.fit_transform(docs)
```

Using the *fit_transform* method, we have created a new vocabulary for the *bag of words* model that transforms the following three sentences into vector features:

1. The weather is amazing

2. The wind is calm

3. The weather is amazing and the wind is calm

Next we need to print the vocabulary content as shown below:

```
>>> print(count.vocabulary_)
```

{'the': 5, 'amazing': 2, 'wind': 6, 'weather': 3, 'is': 1, 'calm': 4,

'and': 0}

The feature vector we created can be represented as follows:

[[0 1 1 1 0 1 0]

[0 1 0 0 1 1 1]

[1 2 1 1 1 2 1]]

Every positional index in our feature vector represents an integer value that can be identified as a dictionary item. In the example above, for example, the values identified in the vector features can be referred to as raw term frequencies.

Determining Relevance

Each time you analyze text data, there is a high likelihood you might come across some words that apply in all the classes across several documents. These words cannot be eliminated because they contain useful information that will help us in classification. To handle such content carefully, we will use the term frequency-inverse document frequency (*tf-idf*) method to determine the weight of such words in our vectors.

If we have the total number of documents as m_d, and *df(d,t)* as the number of documents where the term *t* is used, we must introduce a constant 1 to our denominator so that we do not create a random error. You can refer to the section on overflow and underflow discussed earlier for further explanation.

In Scikit-Learn, we will use the *TfidfTransformer* to convert our raw term frequencies at input into *tf-idf*s as shown below:

> >>> *from sklearn.feature_extraction.text import TfidfTransformer*
>
> >>> *tfidf = TfidfTransformer()*
>
> >>> *np.set_printoptions(precision=2)*
>
> >>> *print(tfidf.fit_transform(count.fit_transform(docs)).toarray())*
>
> *[[0.   0.43 0.56 0.56 0.   0.43 0.]*
>
> *[0.   0.43 0.   0.   0.56 0.43 0.56]*
>
> *[0.4 0.48 0.31 0.31 0.31 0.48 0.31]]*

From here, you can then proceed to cleaning the text data used in the bag of words model. This is important so that you eliminate unnecessary characters from the data. A lot of data present in your text is not necessary for your model, especially the HTML markup information and other non-letter elements like punctuation marks.

> >>> *import re*
>
> >>> *def preprocessor(text):*
>
> ...   *text = re.sub('<[^>]*>', '', text)*
>
> ...   *emoticons = re.findall('(?::|;|=)(?:-)?(?:\)|\(|D|P)', text)*
>
> ...   *text = re.sub('[\W]+', ' ', text.lower()) + *
>
>   *'.join(emoticons).replace('-', '')*

> ...   *return text*

You can clean data using the regular expression library as shown above. This will help us eliminate unnecessary values from the text, which might affect our outcome.

Once you are done with this, the next procedure is to build tokens from the documents we analyze. We will create individual elements from the dataset using the cleaned data as shown below:

> *>>> def tokenizer(text):*
>
> ...   *return text.split()*
>
> *>>> tokenizer('jumpers like jumping and thus they jump')*
>
> *['jumpers', 'like', 'jumping', 'and', 'thus', 'they', 'jump"]*

We must use the bag of words model to train our data before we proceed to the next step. An important procedure here is to remove stop words. Stop words are words that are common in sentences but do not carry any useful information. Therefore, they are irrelevant because we cannot use them to differentiate different document classes. Some common stop words include *has, and,* or *is.*

To eliminate stop words from our movie database, we will use the NLTK library that has a predefined list of 127 stop words. First, we download this list as follows:

> *import nltk*
>
> *nltk.download ('stopwords')*

Next, we use load the instructions as shown below:

>>> *from nltk.corpus import stopwords*

>>> *stop = stopwords.words('english')*

>>> *[w for w in tokenizer_porter('a jumper likes jumping and jumps a*

lot')[-10:] if w not in stop]

['jumper', 'like', 'jump', 'jump', 'lot']

Training a Regression Model

Following through on the data we have prepared so far, we need to train our logistic regression model to determine whether we have positive or negative reviews. For this purpose, we will split the training and test data into two equal sets of 25,000 documents each as shown below:

>>> *X_train = df.loc[:25000, 'review'].values*

>>> *y_train = df.loc[:25000, 'sentiment'].values*

>>> *X_test = df.loc[25000:, 'review'].values*

>>> *y_test = df.loc[25000:, 'sentiment'].values*

From here, the next step is to determine the proper instructions we will use for validation in the logistic regression model. We will have the following code:

```python
>>> from sklearn.grid_search import GridSearchCV
>>> from sklearn.pipeline import Pipeline
>>> from sklearn.linear_model import LogisticRegression
>>> from sklearn.feature_extraction.text import TfidfVectorizer
>>> tfidf = TfidfVectorizer(strip_accents=None,
...                         lowercase=False,
...                         preprocessor=None)
>>> param_grid = [{'vect__ngram_range': [(1,1)],
...
'vect__ngram_range': [(1,1)],
...


>>> lr_tfidf = Pipeline([('vect', tfidf),
...                      ('clf',
...
LogisticRegression(random_state=0))])
>>> gs_lr_tfidf = GridSearchCV(lr_tfidf, param_grid,
...                            scoring='accuracy',
```

...   *cv=5, verbose=1,*

...   *n_jobs=-1)*

>>> gs_lr_tfidf.fit(X_train, y_train)

We will need to determine how accurate our model is. For this, we use the validation accuracy score as follows:

>>> print('CV Accuracy: %.3f'

...   *% gs_lr_tfidf.best_score_)*

CV Accuracy: 0.897

*>>> clf = gs_lr_tfidf.best_estimator_*

>>> print('Test Accuracy: %.3f'

...   *% clf.score(X_test, y_test))*

Test Accuracy: 0.90

Our example reveals a 90% level of accuracy in determining whether reviews are positive or negative.

Analyzing Large Datasets

If there is one thing you might have realized going forward, it is that working with large sets of data is a very expensive affair. Your computer might overheat, or you will realize it is physically struggling when the fan is propelling louder. However, working with huge sets of data is not something you can avoid. Most of the databases you will encounter in real world situations are massive. Since you might not always have access to the best performing computers in the industry, it is wise to find a workaround for such tasks. We can do this through out of core learning as shown in the example below.

In this process, we use an optimization algorithm to determine the weights in the machine learning model, then train our regression model based on tiny fragments of the documents.

We will use a *tokenizer* function to pull and clean data from the CSV file we stored earlier, eliminate stop words and group the words into relative tokens for our task as shown below:

```
>>> import numpy as np

>>> import re

>>> from nltk.corpus import stopwords

>>> stop = stopwords.words('english')

>>> def tokenizer(text):

...     text = re.sub('<[^>]*>', '', text)

...             emoticons = re.findall('(?::|;|=)(?:-)?(?:\)|\(|D|P)',

...                         text.lower())

...     text = re.sub('[\W]+', ' ', text.lower()) \
    + ' '.join(emoticons).replace('-', '')

tokenized = [w for w in text.split() if w not in stop]

return tokenized
```

Remember that we are using the stopwords dictionary fron nltk as outlined earlier. We need a new function that will read data from the movie database and return one document instead of the entire database. For this we use the *stream_docs* generator function as shown:

>>> *def stream_docs(path):*

with open(path, 'r', encoding='utf-8') as csv:

next(csv) # skip header

for line in csv:

text, label = line[:-3], int(line[-2])

yield text, label

Before you proceed, it is important to make sure that the chosen function works as it should. Check to make sure that the first document pulled from the CSV file returns a movie sample and a review, complete with the class label associated with it. This should be in the form of a tuple.

If that checks out, we will create a new function *get_minibatch*. This function will only obtain data from the *stream_docs* and output the number of documents requested in the *size* instruction as shown below:

def get_minibatch(doc_stream, size):

docs, y = [ ], [ ]

try:

for _ in range(size):

```
    text, label = next(doc_stream)

    docs.append(text)

    y.append(label)

except StopIteration:

    return None, None

return docs, y
```

With all the procedures done, we can now finally perform out of core learning as shown below. Remember that we will use the PyPrind library to visualize progress:

```
import pyprind

>>> pbar = pyprind.ProgBar(45)

>>> classes = np.array([0, 1])

>>> for _ in range(45):

X_train, y_train = get_minibatch(doc_stream,
size=1000)

if not X_train:

break

X_train = vect.transform(X_train)

clf.partial_fit(X_train, y_train, classes=classes)

pbar.update ()

0%          100%

ETA[sec]: 0.002
```

Total time elapsed: 49.025 sec

Using the function above, we can obtain the first 3,500 documents to determine how our model performs as shown below:

>>> X_test, y_test = get_minibatch(doc_stream, size=3500)

>>> X_test = vect.transform(X_test)

>>> print('Accuracy: %.3f' % clf.score(X_test, y_test))

Accuracy: 0.871

An 87% accuracy is a good figure, but lower than the accuracy we had achieved earlier. However, take note that this process has taken roughly 49 seconds, which is lower than a minute. We can then use this result to update the model as shown below:

clf = clf.partial_fit(X_test, y_test)

What we have done so far is to use machine learning algorithms to help us classify reviews according to their positive or negative sentiments. An important reminder that you should not forget is that you will work with very large datasets going forward. However, working with them as a whole will exert undue pressure on your computer. Instead of struggling through it, you can simply break down the data using incremental out of core learning to train your machine learning model to work with fragments of data without necessarily bloating the computer memory with the entire dataset. This makes work easier for you, and you don't have to worry about your computer failing you either.

Chapter 7: Natural Language Processing

Machine learning keeps advancing into different industries today. We interact with different models on a daily basis, and it is important to understand how these machines communicate and interpret our instructions. One of the subsets of computer science that addresses this effectively is natural language processing (NLP). Through NLP, computers can easily understand our instructions in the most natural method, and communicate feedback in a way we understand. Without this, we would have to communicate with computers in binary language.

NLP is an important aspect of machine learning because it is the foundation of speech recognition and sentiment analysis. The evolution of NLP over the years has been incredible, given the proliferation of AI mechanisms all over the place. Some of the common instances of NLP that you encounter on a daily basis include AI assistants in your phone like Siri and Cortana, chatbots, and the spell-check assistant in your devices. Machine learning is indeed becoming part and parcel of our lives. To help us understand what NLP is about, let's look at a brief history.

History of Natural Language Processing

NLP is considered, to a wider extent, a class of speech and language processing. As a result, most of the concepts in NLP are similar to computational linguistics and many other studies that involve language processing. Independently, computational linguistics is a branch of study that focuses on using rule-based approaches to understand languages.

The earliest form of NLP with respect to machine learning was recorded in the 1940s. Alongside other evolutionary practices in linguistic studies, this was necessary in the development of formal language theory. Formal language theory basically creates models according to pre existing structures and establishes appropriate rules based on the structures mentioned.

A good example of this is the alphabet. This is a modest structure because it only contains letters which can then be used to create words in the form of letter strings. From this understanding, therefore, we can see a formal language as one that is free of context, but has regular and formal grammatical instructions. NLP builds on this, leveraging its growth on the parallel advancement in technology and widespread access to the Internet and devices connected to the Internet.

Another important concept that helped to champion the growth of NLP is the single-layer perceptron (SLP). This formed the foundation for machine learning and artificial intelligence. SLP is the brainchild of Walter Pitt and Warren McCulloch, logician and neurophysiologist respectively. From their studies, they established the basis for future research in neural networks, most of which are actively in use today like multilayer perceptrons.

Towards the end of the 20th century, studies into NLP advanced into two schools of thought. One group was interested in establishing a symbolic approach to modeling languages, while the other group was keen on championing a stochastic process. As you can imagine the first group was purely supported by linguists. They would come up with simple algorithms that helped them solve basic NLP problems. More often, these solutions involved recognizing patterns and trends in a given set of data.

The second group was supported by engineers and statistical experts. One of the most widely proposed approaches to NLP by engineers and statisticians was the Bayesian statistical approach. Over time, NLP advanced and other aspects were introduced such as natural language understanding. This allowed computers to listen, and understand commands accurately, such that they could react and deliver an expected output.

A good example of natural language understanding is an encounter with a chatbot. If you go online and ask the chatbot to "find nearest schools" it will automatically translate this and return a list of schools close to your location. This means that the computer understands that you need a list of schools, and you need the list to include only schools within your vicinity.

Today, NLP has advanced and integrated into machine learning. NLP is one of the reasons why machine learning is thriving in different industries. For the past 15 years, we have experienced several advancements in the interactions we have with different machine learning models. One of the reasons for this is because massive datasets are available upon which machine learning models train consistently. Models that have interacted with us for 15 years have improved and understand our intentions and actions better and we can see this in the quality of output.

Other than access to massive datasets, we are also at a stage in the computing revolution where we have access to powerful computing resources. Many people have super computers in their homes, yet they barely use a quarter of the resources. Some of the most powerful computers we have today include gaming machines. Beyond their gaming capabilities, these machines can also perform many other tasks, especially if you need them for machine learning purposes.

The resource allocation is an important part of the development of artificial intelligence, and has seen more people interested in learning more about these systems. Besides that, there is an increasing need for data experts, engineers, and scientists to come up with innovative machine learning algorithms that can help solve many of the challenges we struggle to address. From experience, most of the algorithms have been a success. In light of this success, it is only fair that we improve them so that they can learn and advance as our needs do.

NLP In Machine Learning

Having looked at the history of NLP, you can easily understand the hierarchy of processes that we will address in this chapter. You will also understand how NLP works hand in hand with machine learning and deep learning approaches to help in solving unique problems.

There are several machine learning concepts that we will look at in NLP. To help us understand the NLP theories, it is important that we look at issues from a practical approach. In this case, we will use the Python programming language, libraries, and packages. In data science, Python is currently a language that all experts have to learn as it is widely used and adaptable for building scalable applications and solving problems in machine learning.

You will need to brush up on your knowledge of the following Python concepts to help you proceed with this chapter:

- TensorFlow
- Keras

You might also need to learn a bit about Theano, especially if you want to focus on deep learning beyond machine learning concepts.

We will approach NLP with the aim of understanding how machine learning algorithms read, interpret, and respond to text questions. There is always the element of preprocessing involved in interpreting data. In NLP, the common level of preprocessing is to use labels to convert characters into text that can be read by computers. We will look at these concepts in the next section.

There is so much work going on in the field of NLP at the moment that can help us understand how computers process text on the basis of algorithms and implementing functions to classify documents. Let's begin by looking at some of the important features of text processing in the form of feature extraction.

Stop Words and Tokenization

Each time you use some raw data, especially if you obtain data from website crawlers, you collect so much information, some of which is irrelevant to your machine learning needs. Using irrelevant data will only make your work difficult, and in many cases, prevent your machine learning model from working as it should. To avoid this problem, you need to learn how to clean data and eliminate unnecessary input. Let's look at the example below to highlight this:

"'I am a student from Harvard. I was born in Pittsburg, and I love my country.

I want to study Philosophy to so I can become a Philosophy professor. This has been my dream since I was a child.

I am in a PhD program. It is challenging, but I believe I will succeed and this will be the best thing that has ever happened to me."

The computer will print this text as follows

"I am a student from Harvard. I was born in Pittsburg, and I love my country. I want to study Philosophy to so I can become a Philosophy professor. This has been my dream since I was a child. I am in a PhD program. It is challenging, but I believe I will succeed and this will be the best thing that has ever happened to me"

What happens is that your computer will only read the text bodies. It does not matter whether you use string objects or punctuation marks. Our challenge, therefore, is to make sense out of this body of text so that the computer can address all objects as unique string objects. This is where *word tokenization* comes in handy.

Word tokenization is basically a procedure where we identify string objects and separate them from the rest of the unrelated strings. A string object is basically some text in any length that is used to identify characters that we might analyze at a later date. While there are several methods of going about this, the simplest approach is to use the Natural Language Toolkit (NLTK) module.

This module uses some of the key functionalities in NLP to make your work easier. To help you train, we will build our own model based on the data we have. From the earlier example, we should have the following code to tokenize our sample:

```
from nltk.tokenize import word_tokenize, sent_tokenize

sample_word_tokens =
word_tokenize(sample_text)

sample_sent_tokens =
sent_tokenize(sample_text)
```

If we print the sample_word_tokens variable, we should have the output below:

['I' , 'am', 'a', 'student', 'from', 'Harvard', '.', ' 'I', 'was' , 'born', 'in', 'Pittsburg', ',', 'and', 'I', 'love', 'my', 'country', '.', ' 'I', 'want', 'to', 'study', 'Philosophy', 'to', 'so', 'I', 'can', 'become', 'a', 'Philosophy', 'professor', '.', 'This', 'has', 'been', 'my', 'dream', 'since', 'I', 'was', 'a', 'child', '.', 'I', 'am' , 'in', 'a', 'PhD', 'program', '.', 'It', 'is', 'challenging', ',', 'but', 'I' , 'believe' , 'I', 'will', 'succeed', 'and', 'this', 'will', 'be' , 'the', 'best', 'thing', 'that', 'has', 'ever', 'happened', 'to', 'me']

You should also be able to see that we have introduced a tokenized object, sample_sent_tokens. The word_tokenize() and the sent_tokenize() objects are not similar in that the sent_tokenize() uses delimiters to classify sentences. We can see this in the example below:

["I am a student from Harvard. I was born in Pittsburg, and I \nlove my country. I want to study Philosophy to so I can

\nbecome a Philosophy professor. This has been my dream since I \nwas a child. I am in a PhD program. It is challenging, \nbut I believe I will succeed and this will be the best thing that has ever happened to me"]

From our illustration, we can identify unique tokens that can be pre-processed for use. Before we do this, it is important to clean the data and remove any text that is unnecessary. The first group of texts that we must eliminate are the stop words. Stop words are common words used in languages. They do not have any value in terms of the functions we are trying to build, but are only used to establish the grammatical correctness of the sentences.

Some function words that we use in machine learning are also classified as stop words, such as *of, and, for,* and *the.* The NLTK package lists the following stop words in its dictionary:

[u'i', u'me', u'my', u'myself', u'we', u'our', u'ours',

u'ourselves', u'you', u"you're", u"you've", u"you'll",

u"you'd", u'your', u'yours', u'yourself', u'yourselves',

u'he', u'him', u'his', u'himself', u'she', u"she's", u'her',

u'hers', u'herself', u'it', u"it's", u'its', u'itself',

u'they', u'them', u'their', u'theirs', u'themselves', u'what',

u'which', u'who', u'whom', u'this', u'that', u"that'll",

u'these', u'those', u'am', u'is', u'are', u'was', u'were', u'be', u'been', u'being', u'have', u'has', u'had', u'having',

u'do', u'does', u'did', u'doing', u'a', u'an', u'the', u'and',

u'but', u'if', u'or', u'because', u'as', u'until', u'while',

u'of', u'at', u'by', u'for', u'with', u'about', u'against',

u'between', u'into', u'through', u'during', u'before',

u'after', u'above', u'below', u'to', u'from', u'up', u'down',

u'in', u'out', u'on', u'off', u'over', u'under', u'again',

u'further', u'then', u'once', u'here', u'there', u'when',

u'where', u'why', u'how', u'all', u'any', u'both', u'each',

u'few', u'more', u'most', u'other', u'some', u'such', u'no',

u'nor', u'not', u'only', u'own', u'same', u'so', u'than',

u'too', u'very', u's', u't', u'can', u'will', u'just', u'don',

u"don't", u'should', u"should've", u'now', u'd', u'll',

u'm', u'o', u're', u've', u'y', u'ain', u'aren', u"aren't",

u'couldn', u"couldn't", u'didn', u"didn't", u'doesn',

u"doesn't", u'hadn', u"hadn't", u'hasn', u"hasn't", u'haven',

u"haven't", u'isn', u"isn't", u'ma', u'mightn', u"mightn't",

u'mustn', u"mustn't", u'needn', u"needn't", u'shan', u"shan't",

u'shouldn', u"shouldn't", u'wasn', u"wasn't", u'weren',

u"weren't", u'won', u"won't", u'wouldn', u"wouldn't"]

You will also realize that all the stop words in the NLTK dictionary are written in lower case. This is to make sure that when in use, the strings they represent can output true Boolean variables, especially when working on computations to compare strings.

Let's explain this further with an example. Assuming we write a code for *"have" =="HAVE"* our interpreter will return False.

Using the stop words from our example, you can apply the function *mistake()* and *advised_preprocessing()*, and realize that uppercase I characters are ignored by our function.

To solve this problem, you should use uppercase on any stop words that exist within your code. You can do this using the code below:

```
stop_words = [word.upper() for word in
stopwords.

words('english')]

word_tokens = [word for word in
sample_word_tokens if word.

upper() not in stop_words]
```

Make sure your strings match before you apply this code. Besides that, you will also realize that most data comes with a lot of junk information, especially grammatical elements. To make your work easier, the *word_tokenize()* function considers semicolons and colons as unique tokens, though you must still eliminate them from your code. For this reason, NLTK has a tokenizer for that as shown in the example below:

```
from nltk.tokenize import RegexpTokenizer

tokenizer = RegexpTokenizer(r'\w+')

sample_word_tokens                    =
tokenizer.tokenize(str(sample_word_

tokens))

sample_word_tokens = [word.lower() for word
in sample_word_

Tokens]
```

Running this code should eliminate all the standard token words and eliminate grammatical tokens, too. At this point, your document is ready, and you can extract the necessary features for analytical processes.

Bag of Words Model (BoW)

The BoW model is one of the simplest features of machine learning that will help you in feature extraction as you analyze data from time to time. The concept behind this approach is using algorithms that determine how many times a given word is present in your selected text.

In the BoW model, we ignore the order of text and only focus on the frequency of iteration. For example, if we have a container that holds four books, eight pens, and five pencils, our algorithm is only concerned about the number of items in the container, not the order in which they are arranged.

The syntax for a BoW function is as shown below:

```
def bag_of_words(text):

    _bag_of_words                              =
    [collections.Counter(re.findall(r'\w+',

        word)) for word in text]

        bag_of_words    =    sum(_bag_of_words,
        collections.Counter())

        return bag_of_words

sample_word_tokens_bow                         =
bag_of_words(text=sample_word_tokens)

print(sample_word_tokens_bow)
```

If we apply this on the earlier example, it shows us how many times each word is used in the sample. The BoW model returns results as a dictionary function. In as far as machine learning is concerned, a dictionary function is not the best format for input variables. Most algorithms will struggle to interpret this correctly. For this reason, you have to pre-process data. Pre-processing is done using the Scikit-Learn library.

CountVectorizer

The CountVectorizer is almost similar to the BoW, in that text data is represented as a words/feature iteration. All the features are assigned values, which are used to represent the frequency of the words appearing in all the documents within our analytical range. Using the CountVectorizer, we have the code below:

```
from sklearn.feature_extraction.text import CountVectorizer

def bow_sklearn(text=sample_sent_tokens):

    c = CountVectorizer(stop_words='english',

    token_pattern=r'\w+')

    converted_data =
    c.fit_transform(text).todense()

    print(converted_data.shape)

    return                     converted_data,
    c.get_feature_names()
```

Take note that this borrows from the data we defined using the variable *sample_sent_tokens*, and we must also introduce a function for *bow_sklearn()* to indicate the location where we will pre-process data as seen in the code above.

From the code example above our assumption is that all the sentences are unique documents. Therefore, if you have 673 sentences, we assume you are working with 673 documents. From this understanding, you will also build a set of features where every single feature is considered an independent token.

The *CountVectorizer()* function includes the parameters *token_pattern* and *stop_words*, which are important in eliminating grammatical tokens and stop words, and in feature extraction.

The attribute *fit_transform()* tells us the kind of object that the model expects to receive. This could be a list, an iterable string of objects, or even an array. The result from our code should represent a matrix of values, based on how many times they appear in the content.

Term Frequency Inverse Document Frequency (TFIDF)

Term frequency inverse document frequency is built on the understanding of BoW. However, unlike BoW, it gives us more information beyond identifying the frequency of iterations. The TFIDF will not just tell us how many times some words are repeated in our content, it will also reveal their values, thereby informing us of how important the specific words are. This is where term frequency is important, and we can see an example below:

> *"I was a student at the University of Manchester, but now work on*
>
> *Apple as a Lawyer. I have been living in London for roughly four years*
>
> *now, however I am looking forward to eventually retiring to Illinois once I have enough savings."*

To define the context of the text above, we will use the following code:

$$document\_list = list([sample\_text, text])$$

This should return a list of documents as expected. So, what does the TFIDF algorithm do? There are two segments of the TFIDF algorithm, the term frequency, and the inverse document frequency. The first segment can be expressed in several ways. However, at this juncture we are more interested in the standard raw count. In this case, we will add up all the terms present in the documents. We should have the code below:

```
def tf_idf_example(textblobs=[text, text2]):

def term_frequency(word, textblob): (1)

return
textblob.words.count(word)/float(len(textblob.
words))

def document_counter(word, text):

return sum(1 for blob in text if word in blob)

def idf(word, text): (2)

return          np.log(len(text)          /1          +
float(document_counter(word,

text)))

def tf_idf(word, blob, text):

return term_frequency(word, blob) * idf(word,
text)

output = list()

for i, blob in enumerate(textblobs):
```

```
output.append({word:     tf_idf(word,     blob,
textblobs) for word in

blob.words})

print(output)
```

Based on our example above, we should have a 2 x 44 matrix outcome, which we will use as input into our machine learning model for analysis.

Each time you analyze some data using these methods, there is always an outside possibility that your training data might be overfit. However, for the best performance, you need to ensure that the test data is as close to your logistical regression data as possible. Why as close as possible? This is because it is almost impossible to maintain the same level of accuracy in both sets of data, given that they both experience different computations.

As you analyze data resulted from the random forest and Naive Bayes classifiers, you will notice that the accuracy scores are almost similar. However, there might be a slight difference in the true positives and false positives, which we can ignore as we proceed with the model. The most important thing at this juncture is to ensure that you keep your objective for building the model in mind. It is easy to get carried away when you are in control of data manipulation, to the point where you build an amazing model but it is so far from what the original intentions were.

In the examples we used for the IMDb database, we use algorithms to understand the kind of reviews that users give about the movies they watched. From these reviews, we can then conduct an analytical process that will help us maximize the level of accuracy, determine results that have the highest rate of positive scores and those with a high rate of negative scores. Using this knowledge in spam filtration models for example, our objective will be trying to select a model that can identify spam mail from regular mail.

The good thing about using the BoW model is that it is so easy, you can implement it in both the Naive Bayes classifiers and logistic algorithm models. You should also know the benefits and challenges involved in using any approach, so that you do not end up spending a lot of time trying to find solutions with methods that are not useful.

BoW is simple and straightforward. It should not take you a long time to convert text into an interpretable format for analysis in machine learning. You can use this to find solutions to NLP problems faster than any other approach available.

However, the biggest pitfall of the BoW approach is its fair simplicity. There are many elements of data that are important but are ignored by BoW. For example, this approach does not consider the context of words used in the data. Because of this reason, it is not necessarily the best approach to use for feature extraction, especially when you are dealing with relatively complicated NLP assignments.

To elaborate this further, in semantic consideration, "3" and "three" should mean the same thing. However, in BoW, these are two independent words with different meanings.

Another example is "I studied Medicine for five years in college", and "For 5 years at the university, I studied Medicine". BoW considers these two statements as orthogonal vector statements. This also introduces another challenge with BoW - it cannot determine the order of words. Therefore, BoW will consider the following statements as an identical vector "I am hungry" and "Am I hungry".

Looking at these challenges, it is important that you learn to work with advanced models over time. Find difficult problems that push the limit of your knowledge in machine learning. The more you try working with complex problems, the easier it will be for you to handle similar challenges in the future.

It is important that you learn NLP because the knowledge gained will be useful when solving a wide range of problems. In your capacity as a data analyst or a programmer, you will realize that you encounter challenges in varied domains. Because of this reason, it is always a good idea to know the best method to use and arrive at the optimal solution faster.

Some concepts that you learn in NLP will apply in different aspects of machine learning. Of special mention here is data preprocessing. You must always ensure your data exists within the right framework and structure for your model. Without this, you might not be able to build the right model. To be precise, most of the data used in machine learning that makes it difficult for many people to understand comes from preprocessed data. There are a lot of mistakes that data handlers and anyone else involved in preparing data can make, which affect your results in the long run.

When working on a solution for similar problems, the steps to preprocessing might be similar in most cases. However, you must still exercise caution when handling such problems so that you can build the appropriate solution going forward.

A common mistake that many programmers make is to focus on the programming part and ignore the data handling process. As a rule of thumb, never trust the integrity of any data presented to you, unless there are measures in place to ensure the data is correct. Unless you suffer time constraints, spare some time and go through any data you should use before you introduce it into your model. You must exercise caution and be responsible in the way you collect and process data, irrespective of the programming environment you use.

Once you cover the basics, you will realize that neural networks, common in NLP, are very easy to operate and implement in different programming models. Perhaps the challenge that you might have is determining the correct input data and the predictive capacity of the said data. Other than that, the only challenge you should struggle with, especially when working with a massive set of data, is how to structure it in a manner that your machine learning model can identify trends and patterns that can be exploited.

As you build machine learning models based on NLP, you must also know the perfect time to train or retrain your models without committing resources unnecessarily. The best approach is to use live data. The good thing with using live data is that you can always monitor the model's performance and know when it is depreciating. When you realize a slump in performance, it is time to refresh the model and retrain it.

Retraining your model is not the final process. Make sure you document the procedure followed in retraining your model, and at the same time, ensure you are aware of the effect of the training process on performance, accuracy, speed of deriving outcomes, and any other measurable features. You need these notes to determine whether retraining improved the overall performance of your machine learning model or not. You must also look at the changes in performance in terms of your computer resources. Is your computer struggling to process data after the retraining? Look at the performance indicators in the task manager. This will show you how much memory is consumed before the retraining, during, and after. This information can also help you determine whether you need to invest in better computing equipment or not.

Even if you build a model that is perfect and persistent in operation, retraining is never a guarantee that things will be easier. This is why documentation helps, so that you can trace your steps in retraining the model and probably identify errors in your process.

Chapter 8: Loading Machine Learning Models into Real World Applications

Over the course of these books you have learned so much about machine learning, from introduction, taxonomies, and how to work with algorithms. At the beginning of this book we mentioned that we will work on real world examples to give you a true feeling of what it feels like to work with machine learning models. There is no better way to do this than loading your successful model onto normal applications that people use all the time. After all, once the model has passed the testing and evaluation stage, it is high time it meets the world, right?

The models you build should never be confined to theoretical and offline analytics. They are built to engage with the world, to provide solutions to problems. We mentioned how to build a spam detection filter earlier. Having proven that the filter is perfect, why not load it into a web application and see how well it performs? There are many other machine learning models that you can build. Each of these models will, eventually, go live. In this section, we will look at the most important part of your work: how to integrate your model into the real world.

Model Training

You might have realized this by now, that training a machine learning model is not exactly a cheap affair. If you think about the resource consumption, you cannot afford to train the model every time you terminate your Python interpreter session. If you do this, you will also need to make new predictions each time you start your web applications. An easier way around this is to use the in-built pickle module to boost the persistence of your machine learning model.

Through the pickle module, you can serialize Python structures accordingly, such that each time you close the program, the classifier is saved in its present running state. When you run it again, it does not have to start relearning the model through training data to remember what it's supposed to do. This saves you on resources and time.

Before you proceed, you should refresh your memory on out of core logistic regression training because this will help you save time and understand the examples used here faster.

In the example below, we will use data from the CSV file from IMDb database. You should have the following code ready:

```
>>> import pickle

>>> import os

>>> dest = os.path.join('movieclassifier', 'pkl_objects')

>>> if not os.path.exists(dest):

... os.makedirs(dest)

>>> pickle.dump(stop,

...                          open(os.path.join(dest, 'stopwords.pkl'),'wb'),
```

```
...         protocol=4)

>>> pickle.dump(clf,

...             open(os.path.join(dest, 'classifier.pkl'),
'wb'),

...         protocol=4)
```

In this example, we have introduced a new directory path, *movieclassifier*. We shall use this directory to store data and files from our web app. You might have realized by now that the regression algorithm model we use has a lot of NumPy arrays. To ensure that these arrays are compatible, we can use a standard pickle method as shown below:

```
from        sklearn.feature_extraction.text        import
HashingVectorizer

import re

import os

import pickle

cur_dir = os.path.dirname(__file__)

stop = pickle.load(open(

        os.path.join(cur_dir,

        'pkl_objects',

        'stopwords.pkl'), 'rb'))

def tokenizer(text):

    text = re.sub('<[^>]*>', '', text)
```

```python
    emoticons        =        re.findall('(?::|;|=)(?:-
)?(?:\)|\(|D|P)',

            text.lower())

    text = re.sub('[\W]+', ' ', text.lower()) \

        + ' '.join(emoticons).replace('-', '')

    tokenized = [w for w in text.split() if w not
in stop]

    return tokenized

vect                                =
HashingVectorizer(decode_error='ignore',

        n_features=2**21,

        preprocessor=None,

        tokenizer=tokenizer)
```

Ensure you are using data from a secure source to protect your devices. Some sources usually contain harmful code so be very careful.

Launch a new session on Python and use the code below to determine whether you can import and unpickle the data as required:

```python
>>> import pickle

>>> import re

>>> import os

>>> from vectorizer import vect

>>> clf = pickle.load(open(
```

```
...        os.path.join('pkl_objects',

...                  'classifier.pkl'), 'rb'))
```

Once you load the samples, you can use the content within to make predictions based on different values. Classifiers in our examples should deliver integral class labels. This is why it is important to use Python dictionaries. This way, we can assign integers to specific sentiments, so that when we review the results, we understand what it is about.

```
>>> import numpy as np

>>> label = {0:'negative', 1:'positive'}

>>> example = ['I loved the movie']

>>> X = vect.transform(example)

>>> print('Prediction:    %s\nProbability: %.2f%%' %\

...      (label[clf.predict(X)[0]],

...      np.max(clf.predict_proba(X))*100))

Prediction: positive

Probability: 92.47%
```

We managed to transform document content into a vector using the Hashing vectorizer, while the *predict_proba* method in logistic regression will tell us the probability that our prediction is true or false.

Data Storage in SQLite

We need as much feedback as possible from our model to determine whether it is accurate. For this reason, it is wise to collect as much information as necessary to satisfy our assertions. It is based on such feedback that we can analyze and update our machine learning model to meet the user needs and demands.

A useful tool for this process is the SQLite database engine. This is an open-source platform so you do not need to run another server to use it. For this reason, it is a useful resource, especially when you are working on a small project or if you are building a relatively small application that does not need a standalone server.

From the SQLite database engine, you should be able to access stored files without any challenges. Besides, this engine does not demand any specific configurations unique to operating systems, so you can use it without any restrictions. It is available in the Python library through the API sqlite3, so you should have an easier time with this.

Now, we need to establish a new database in the movie classifier directory using SQLite. In this directory, we will hold two types of reviews, a positive and a negative one as shown below:

```
>>> import sqlite3

>>> import os

>>> conn = sqlite3.connect('reviews.sqlite')

>>> c = conn.cursor()

>>> c.execute('CREATE TABLE review_db'\
```

```
...              ' (review TEXT, sentiment INTEGER,
date TEXT)')

>>> example1 = 'I love the movie'

>>> c.execute("INSERT INTO review_db"\

...           " (review, sentiment, date) VALUES"\

...           " (?, ?, DATETIME('now'))", (example1,
1))

>>> example2 = 'I hate the movie'

>>> c.execute("INSERT INTO review_db"\

...           " (review, sentiment, date) VALUES"\

...           " (?, ?, DATETIME('now'))", (example2,
0))

>>> conn.commit()

>>> conn.close()
```

We should determine whether all the entries are properly stored in our database. To do this, we will use the SQL commands to identify rows which are committed between specific dates. At this juncture, you can also see why the DATETIME command is relevant. By adding timestamps, you can pull data from the database between specific timelines. If your timestamp is *now*, the system will automatically assume the current time in your timezone, and use this as a relevant measure where applicable. The code below will help you determine whether all entries are correct in the database:

```
>>> conn = sqlite3.connect('reviews.sqlite')

>>> c = conn.cursor()
```

```
>>> c.execute("SELECT * FROM review_db
WHERE date"\

...     " BETWEEN '2018-01-01 00:00:00' AND
DATETIME('now')")

>>> results = c.fetchall()

>>> conn.close()

>>> print(results)
```

[('I love the movie', 1, '2019-10-03 16:00:10'), ('I hated the

movie', 0, '2019-10-03 16:00:10')]

The instructions above try to ascertain the validity of entries in our database by pulling data from 2018 to the current date. You can also request information between specific timelines, not necessarily up to the current date.

Say you needed data between 2017 and 2018, you will have the following code:

```
>>> conn = sqlite3.connect('reviews.sqlite')

>>> c = conn.cursor()

>>> c.execute("SELECT * FROM review_db
WHERE date"\

...     " BETWEEN '2017-01-01 00:00:00' AND
DATETIME('now')")

>>> results = c.fetchall()

>>> conn.close()
```

```
>>> print(results)

[('I love the movie', 1, '2018-01-01 00:00:00'),
('I hated the

movie', 0, '2018-01-01 00:00:00')]
```

Building Web Apps

What we have done so far is to prepare our data such that we can derive information at specific intervals. We no longer need to go through the cumbersome and resource intensive process of uploading the entire database. Instead, we can use specific instructions to obtain data between a given timeline.

The next process is to build a web app. An important tool that will help in this process is Flask. Flask is a framework that has been around since 2010 and has been used in some of the most successful projects to date such as Pinterest.

Luckily for programmers, Flask is written in Python, so you should not struggle to integrate your work into it, especially if you have extensive knowledge of Python. Check to see whether your Python environment has Flask installed. If not, you can install it from the terminal as shown below:

pip install flask

To understand the Flask API, we can create a simple application that we will then use in with the movie database we have studied extensively.

my_flask_app/

app.py

templates/

first_app.html

All the code you need for this process is stored in the *app.py* file. This is the file your Python interpreter executes to run the web app you build on Flask. You should have the following code from your render template:

```
app = Flask(__name__)

@app.route('/') #specifies the URL to execute

def index():

    return render_template('first_app.html')

if __name__ == '__main__':

    app.run()
```

Just like you did when writing your first HTML code, we follow the same process in Flask. The syntax is similar as shown below:

```
<!doctype html>

<html>

 <head>

  <title>Flask App</title>

 </head>

 <body>
```

```
<div>Hello World, meet my Flask web
app!</div>

</body>

</html>
```

One of the best things about using Flask is that you can render your apps locally. This is a brilliant idea because it helps you build and test applications before you run them live on a public server. This allows you enough room to experiment and ensure your code is perfect.

Next, we will run the code within the *my_flask_app* directory. Since you are using the local server, you should see the local server address when you run *python app.py* as shown below:

Running on http://128.0.0.152/

To display progress as you work on the app, copy and paste this address into your web browser. Assuming everything is running as it should, your browser should display the following content:

Hello World, meet my Flask web app!

Next we will introduce some HTML form elements to obtain data from users. The WTForms library is a good solution for this stage. Install it as shown below:

pip install wtforms

This creates a text field where users can input their details. For example, the text prompt will request as follows:

Prompt: What's Your Name?

Text box: Andrei

Prompt: Say Hello

Text Box: Hello Andrei

When you click on the submission prompt *Say Hello,* your form will validate and create a new HTML page that renders the details entered.

The directory we have built up to this level should look like this in your code:

my_flask_app_2/

app.py

static/

style.css

templates/

_formhelpers.html

first_app.html

hello.html

We can then create a CSS file to modify the look and feel of our data as shown below:

body {

font-size: 12;

}

Our first_app.html file should contain the following features:

<!doctype html>

<html>

```html
<head>

<title>Flask App</title>

<link rel="stylesheet" href="{{ url_for('static',

filename='style.css') }}">

</head>

<body>

{% from "_formhelpers.html" import
render_field %}

<div>What's your name?</div>

<form method=post action="/hello">

<dl>

{{ render_field(form.sayhello) }}

</dl>

<input type=submit value='Say Hello'
name='submit_btn'>

</form>

</body>

</html>
```

We have loaded the CSS file into the header of our document. As a result, all the text features in the document have changed. Finally, we create a *hello.html* file to render within the *hello* function. Our code should look like this:

```html
<!doctype html>
```

```
<html>

  <head>

    <title>Flask App</title>

    <link rel="stylesheet" href="{{ url_for('static',

    filename='style.css') }}">

    </head>

    <body>

    <div>Hello {{ name }}</div>

    </body>

  </html>
```

In so doing, we have created a simple web application on Flask that runs locally at *http://128.0.0.152/*

Converting Classifiers into Web Apps

Now that you already know how to use Flask, we can breeze through the next session and convert our movie classifier into a web application. Our task is to build a web app that will first prompt the user to name the movie they want to review.

After submitting their review, the user can then see a page that identifies the class label and their prediction probability. You can add more functions to the app, such as allowing users to confirm whether their review is accurate or not. You can also allow the user to submit more reviews.

Following the movie database review, you should have a *vectorizer.py* file in your SQLite database. Check the directory to ensure you have it. One of the challenges you will have with the *app.py* file is its size. This file is characteristically long. Therefore, you can handle it in two ways. First, you import Python objects and modules necessary for the machine learning classification model as shown below:

```
from flask import Flask, render_template, request

from wtforms import Form, TextAreaField, validators

import pickle

import sqlite3

import os

import numpy as np


app = Flask(__name__)
# Prepares the Classifier
cur_dir = os.path.dirname(__file__)
clf = pickle.load(open(os.path.join(cur_dir,
        'pkl_objects/classifier.pkl'), 'rb'))
db = os.path.join(cur_dir, 'reviews.sqlite')
def classify(document):
    label = {0: 'negative', 1: 'positive'}
```

```
X = vect.transform([document])

y = clf.predict(X)[0]

proba = clf.predict_proba(X).max()

return label[y], proba

def train(document, y):

    X = vect.transform([document])

    clf.partial_fit(X, [y])


def sqlite_entry(path, document, y):

    conn = sqlite3.connect(path)

    c = conn.cursor()

    c.execute("INSERT    INTO    review_db
(review, sentiment, date)"\

    " VALUES    (?,    ?,    DATETIME('now'))",
(document, y))

    conn.commit()

    conn.close()
```

After this, you must create a classify function that returns prediction probabilities against the associated class labels as shown below:

```
app = Flask(__name__)

class ReviewForm(Form):

    moviereview = TextAreaField('',
```

```python
                    [validators.DataRequired(),

                    validators.length(min=15)])

@app.route('/')

def index():

    form = ReviewForm(request.form)

    return render_template('reviewform.html',
form=form)

    @app.route('/results', methods=['POST'])

    def results():

        form = ReviewForm(request.form)

        if request.method == 'POST' and
form.validate():

            review = request.form['moviereview']

            y, proba = classify(review)

            return render_template('results.html',

                        content=review,

                        prediction=y,

probability=round(proba*100, 2))

        return render_template('reviewform.html',
form=form)

    @app.route('/thanks', methods=['POST'])

    def feedback():
```

```
feedback = request.form['feedback_button']

review = request.form['review']

prediction = request.form['prediction']

inv_label = {'negative': 0, 'positive': 1}

y = inv_label[prediction]

if feedback == 'Incorrect':

    y = int(not(y))

train(review, y)

sqlite_entry(db, review, y)

return render_template('thanks.html')

if __name__ == '__main__':

app.run(debug=True)
```

In the final HTML file, you can request users to suggest another review, or confirm whether their feedback is correct or not as shown below:

```
<!doctype html>

<html>

<head>

<title>Movie Classification</title>

</head>

<body>

<h3>Thank you for your review!!</h3>
```

```
<div id='button'>

<form action="/">

<input type=submit value='Review another
movie">

</form>

</div>

</body>

</html>
```

We have looked at several features that are useful in machine learning. Most of the concepts usually seem complicated at first glance, but after further prodding, you realize they are not as difficult as they seem. In most cases, the challenge comes when you are dealing with very large datasets.

Conclusion

For all that we know about machine learning, the truth is that we are nowhere close to realizing the true potential of these studies. Machine learning is currently one of the hottest topics in computer science. If you are a data analyst, this is a field you should focus all your energy on because the prospects are incredible. You are looking at a future where interaction with machines will form the base of our being.

In this installation, our purpose was to address Python machine learning from the perspective of an expert. The assumption is that you have gone through the earlier books in the series that introduced you to machine learning, Python, libraries, and other important features that form the foundation of your knowledge in machine learning. With this in mind, we barely touched on the introductory concepts, unless necessary.

Even at an expert level it is always important to remind yourself of the important issues that we must look at in machine learning. Algorithms are the backbone of almost everything that you will do in machine learning. Because of this reason, we introduced a brief section where you can remind yourself of the important algorithms and other elements that help you progress your knowledge of machine learning.

Machine learning is as much about programming as it is about probability and statistics. There are many statistical approaches that we will use in machine learning to help us arrive at optimal solutions from time to time. It is therefore important that you remind yourself about some of the necessary probability theories and how they affect outcomes in each scenario.

In our studies of machine learning from the beginner books through intermediary level to this point, one concept that stands out is that machine learning involves uncertainty. This is one of the differences between machine learning and programming. In programming, you write code that must be executed as it is written. The code derives a predetermined output based on the instructions given. However, in machine learning, this is not a luxury we enjoy.

Once you build the model, you train and test it and eventually deploy the model. Since these models are built to interact with humans, you can expect variances in the type of interaction that you experience at every level. Some input parameters might be correct, while others might not. When you build your model, you must take these factors into consideration, or your model will cease to perform as expected.

The math element of machine learning is another area of study that we have to look at. We didn't touch on this so much in the earlier books in the series because it is an advanced level study. There are many mathematical computations that are involved in machine learning in order for the models to deliver the output we need. To support this cause, we must learn how to perform specific operations on data based on unique instructions.

As you work with different sets of data, there is always the possibility that you will come across massive datasets. This is normal because as our machine learning models interact with different users, they keep learning and build their knowledge. The challenge with using massive datasets is that you must learn how to break down the data into small units that your system can handle and process without any challenges. In this case, you are trying to avoid overworking your learning model.

Most basic computers will crash when they have to handle massive data. However, this should not be a problem when you learn how to fragment your datasets and perform computational operations on them.

At the beginning of this book we mentioned that we will introduce hands-on approaches to using machine learning in daily applications. In light of this assertion, we looked at some practical methods of using machine learning, such as building a spam filter, and analyzing a movie database.

We have taken a careful step-by-step approach to ensure that you can learn along the way, and more importantly, tried to explain each process to help you understand the operations you perform and why.

Eventually, when you build a machine learning model, the aim is to integrate it into some of the applications that people use on a daily basis. With this in mind, it is important that you learn how to build a simple solution that addresses this challenge. We used simple explanations to help you understand this, and hopefully as you keep working on different machine learning models, you can learn by building more complex models as your needs permit.

There are many concepts in machine learning that you will learn or come across over time. You must reckon the fact that this is a never-ending learning process as long as your model interacts with data. Over time, you will encounter greater datasets than those you are used to working with. In such a scenario, learning how to handle them will help you achieve your results faster, and without struggling.

References

Andrew L. Maas, Raymond E. Daly, Peter T. Pham, Dan Huang, Andrew Y. Ng, and Christopher Potts. (2011). Learning Word Vectors for Sentiment Analysis. The 49th Annual Meeting of the Association for Computational Linguistics (ACL 2011).

www.ingramcontent.com/pod-product-compliance
Lightning Source LLC
Chambersburg PA
CBHW071133050326
40690CB00008B/1446